VOLUME ONE

TOP STARS OF NASCAR VOLUME I

Bob Schaller, Top Stars of NASCAR Volume I

ISBN 1-887002-89-X

Cross Training Publishing
317 West Second Street
Grand Island, NE 68801
(308) 384-5762
Copyright © 1999 by Cross Training Publishing

Research for "Top Stars of NASCAR" was done from more than a hundred news-papers, periodicals and online services, including Knight-Ridder News Service, Scripps Howard News Service, Gannett News Service, NASCAR Winston Cup Scene, NASCAR Winston Cup Illustrated, and ESPN, TNN Motorsports, Fox Sports, TBS Motorsports, CNNSI, MRN Radio and the weekly media teleconfer-ences, including the MCI Teleconference, NASCAR Trucks, USA Today, Sports Illustrated, various sponsors and marketing groups provided press releases and race/news comments from drivers, and CBS SportsLine, ESPN SportsZone, Fox Sports, goracing.com, iRACE, Racing Zone, SpeedNet, Speedworld, That's Racin' and NASCAR Online. NASCAR Online, which provides online chats open to all fans and media, is setting the pace for all sports online reporting services, so go to NASCAR Online and stay on the lead lap of NASCAR coverage. Check out www.nascar.com for the latest racing news, features, points standings, schedules and profiles, updated faster than a short-track pit stop.

Published by Cross Training Publishing
317 West Second Street
Grand Island, NE 68801
1-800-430-8588

Photo Credit:
Fellowship of Christian Athletes

TABLE OF CONTENTS

Like many others, I was caught off-guard when the NASCAR bug bit me. I am not in "NASCAR's inner circle," so these comments simply come from a fan who happens to be a writer. In this book, and in the following editions (Volume II and Volume III), you will get to read about the drivers who make this sport the fastest growing one in the world.

Of course, as a sports editor for more than a decade at a daily newspaper, I was familiar with racing. But that just scratches the surface as to what NASCAR is all about, and it doesn't do justice to everything NASCAR entails, from strong values and an emphasis on family to teamwork and outstanding sportsmanship.

However, there are also several tangible reasons why NASCAR has become the fastest growing sport in the world in terms of fan popularity, and here are a dozen. In keeping with NASCAR's classy approach, I will focus only on NASCAR, while not taking shots at any other sports (which I also enjoy, but pale in comparison to NASCAR).

1. Every single race matters: Unlike a lot of professional sports where games later in the season may not affect the team's standing, every race matters in NASCAR. Drivers are constantly jockeying to move up in the points standings. Indeed, winning the points standing is like NASCAR's version of the Super Bowl or World Series. However, unlike those events, NASCAR's championship is literally decided on a week-to-week basis. Since a crash or mechanical problem can knock a driver back more than one hundred points, each week takes on special significance, which is among the reasons why there are more than 100,000 fans at each race.

2. Drivers must perform on a weekly, even daily, basis: This keeps drivers "hungry"—their workweek never ends. Either they are trying to qualify for a race, or they are testing a track for a race down the road. And when race time comes, they have to perform. There are no long-term bazillion-dollar contracts like the ones that exist for prima donna athletes in other sports. In NASCAR, you are only as good as your last race—until the next green flag drops on the

following week's race. There is no "coasting"—literally—in NASCAR. Either a driver goes all out every week, or he/she won't have a ride for the following season.

3. These drivers have courage: This is something often lacking in other sports. Look at a "disabled" list for other sports, and you will find athletes missing action with a slight muscle pull or even a hangnail in extreme cases. NASCAR drivers compete with broken limbs and other physical woes. That desire, heart and courage is appreciated by the fans. You and I can't draw million-dollar salaries because our hamstring is a little sore, and neither can NASCAR drivers. Even if your driver is in a crash one week, don't be surprised to see that driver out on the track the following week. Along those lines, NASCAR and its teams do have the common sense to support a driver who needs time off for a serious injury, such as a concussion. The sponsors and team owners in NASCAR have set a new standard for supporting their drivers because they know no driver will simply "take a day off" unless it is medically recommended.

4. As a "racing" sport, NASCAR is the most entertaining of any: Watching the open-wheel Indy cars fly around the track can get old after, say, the first few laps. Indeed, the fragile Indy cars, traveling at 200-plus miles an hour, can't so much as tap each other because it produces almost the same effect as a plane crash, with vehicle parts flying in every direction. In NASCAR, bumping and "swapping paint" happens regularly. The cars and trucks are constructed in such a manner that the close quarters don't take away from the race, and, in fact, actually add to the race as the drivers push each other to get better track position or pass. At the same time, the sportsmanship level is so high that drivers avoid spinning each other out simply for self gain. And if it does happen, the guilty driver will usually admit it and apologize to the other drivers.

5. Not just the winner of a race "wins" on a given day: With the points battle being waged throughout the season, if your driver does not win the race, his finishing position still matters—that is, not winning does not mean a loss. No driver is going to win every race;

that's why statistics such as "top-five" and "top-10" finishes mean so much.

6. The different tracks: NASCAR has its own version of "expansion," but it doesn't mean "giving" a city a team and a clever name and logo. NASCAR expands by exploring new markets, as it has done with adding races in Arizona, California and Texas. NASCAR's management is so aware of its fans and their importance that it is constantly casting an open-minded eye at new race venues. Expansion also comes yearly through new teams and drivers at every level—the Winston Cup, Busch Grand National and Craftsman Truck series. The Winston Cup is the premier level, and drivers from both the Busch and Trucks series usually set a goal to one day run in the Cup. Since the Busch Grand Nationals and Craftsman Trucks are far more exciting and better marketed than other sports' "minor" leagues, all three series have solid fan bases.

7. Every moment of a race matters: Some sports have "down times" where the game is not really hanging in the balance. That's not the case in a NASCAR race. The first few laps are crucial as drivers find their comfort level with their cars and what adjustments need to be made, while avoiding the wrecks that are more likely to occur at the start when there are 40 vehicles in the race. Pit strategy can win or lose a race for a driver, making every second—even every one-tenth of a second—important on pit row. The pits are a battle in themselves, with teams deciding whether to replace two tires or four, how many adjustments to make on a car, etc. Championships are, to be sure, won by great drivers, yet no driver, no matter how great, can win without a great pit crew. That kind of teamwork— every person doing his job at the highest possible level at every moment—keeps the race exciting at every single moment. Furthermore, the pit strategy extends from when and how to pit to computing fuel mileage. Many times a driver can get back into a race—or fall from contention—by being aware of fuel mileage. That's why NASCAR fans are so sophisticated—because so many phases of the race matter, fans are more involved, watching to see which team excels in every facet.

8. Different stops, different vehicles—something for everyone: There are the fastest of the fastest cars on the Winston Cup, a sort of feeder league in the Busch Grand National Series, and the Craftsman Trucks, which also has provided several top Winston Cup drivers. All three have their own followings, and all are exciting. The different kinds of tracks—superspeedway, short tracks and road courses—provide fans with a different "playing field" to watch each week. Plus, the different states and cities give fans in almost every area an opportunity to catch their favorite drivers in action, whether in qualifying or in the actual race.

9. You can root for more than one driver: In most team sports, one team wins and another loses. In NASCAR, it is just not that way. A driver who is in, say, 10th place in the point standings can be greatly helped by a top-five finish, just as drivers nearing the top 20 or top 30 can leap in the standings by a high placing. Many fans have several favorite drivers, so no race is ever a total disappointment because at least one or two of their favorites will help themselves. At the same time, fans can follow drivers peripherally and can chart if a driver is on the upswing or downturn. In no other sport is a team or driver more constantly open to evaluation.

10. NASCAR is a great sport for the family: Drivers bring their families to races. Many of the drivers participate very actively in the Christian ministry the tour has built up over the years. These drivers take their role model status very seriously and seem very proud to be in the public eye. In NASCAR, drivers are committed to their families and their teams and do all they can to represent both— along with NASCAR itself—in the most positive manner possible. That leaves NASCAR alone atop the professional sports heap in what is, especially in this day and age, a very important category to fans, especially parents. And these drivers/teams/owners are doing something for various charities every week, making it so everyone associated with NASCAR feels like a winner.

11. There is simply no more fan-friendly sport than NASCAR: The drivers and crew members are always open to sign autographs.

The drivers truly care for their sponsors and team owners, and it is shown when they thank them at every turn. How many million-dollar athletes have been in very public fights with their team owner or coach/manager? That hardly ever happens in NASCAR. And that is part of the appeal. Also, sponsors are known and recognized as being a part of the team—indeed, they are actually referred to as the "team"—the Halvoline Ford driven by Mark Martin, the Dupont Chevy driven by Jeff Gordon, the Interstate Batteries Pontiac of Bobby Labonte, Ron Hornaday's NAPA truck, and on down the line. In many sports, the sponsors' presence is on a stadium wall and can be perceived as more of an annoyance than anything else. In NASCAR, the sponsor is very much a part of the sport's flavor and provides a means by which fans watching the race can identify cars or trucks.

12. NASCAR, the governing body, makes the right decisions: Whether it is putting the fans first, making sure their drivers and teams are safe, or in terms of marketing, NASCAR has set a standard that other pro sports can only dream about reaching. NASCAR made some of its drivers a little edgy by requiring "restrictor plates" at superspeedways to keep the cars from going over 200 miles an hour. Some of the drivers have expressed frustration with that because their competitiveness makes them want to go faster and faster. But NASCAR is concerned about driver and fan safety, and the restrictor-plate requirement, while not always popular, was done with the right intention and with respect for everyone—the drivers, owners and fans. On top of that, the broadcasts by ESPN, TNN and TBS have set another standard no sport will ever reach. Cameras in the car not only give the fans a great view, but explain why things unfold the way they do, from passing cars to accidents. The on-board telemetry shows how fast drivers go and how hard they are running the cars, which also gives fans the thrill of being "in the car" and explains why some cars are doing better than others. The pit row reporting puts the fans "in the pits" and lets the fans know why certain things happen, something that will likely always be missing in other sports. The race

announcers, many of whom are former drivers, offer sincere insights that keep a fan excited and informed. In short, NASCAR is simply a lap ahead of the other professional sports.

CHAPTER 1

JOHN ANDRETTI

Andretti's answers: First career pole came in the 1995 Mountain Dew Southern 500 at Darlington; scored first NASCAR Winston Cup Series win in 1997 Pepsi 400 at Daytona.

John Andretti has wins to his credit in IndyCar and IMSA racing, along with just about all other kinds of racing; from drag to midgets and dirt and sprint cars, he's been a winner. In 1996, Andretti had a pair of top-10 Winston Cup finishes and finished the season 31st in points. Andretti, the nephew of racing legend Mario (John's father, Aldo, is Mario's twin brother), has a degree from Moravia College (with honors, a major in business management).

Andretti and his father had a lot of quality time together early in John's racing career.

"My dad and I spent every day until I quit racing go-karts, which was right before I went to college, working in the garage together," said Andretti, who was born March 12, 1963. "So our relationship is really tight.

"I played football, baseball and basketball just like every other little kid, and my dad, being from Italy, didn't know the rules or anything, so he didn't have much interest in those sports," Andretti said. "Not that he didn't have interest in what we were doing—he just didn't know what was going on. Racing is something that he knew. Actually, it was my mom who suggested we go racing, since it was something my older brother, Mark, and my dad and I could do together. So we went off and did it, just for fun. We both got hurt the same day in different incidents on the track right in front of my mom. After that it took a while to get going again and talk her back into letting us race."

Aside from racing, one of Andretti's greatest joys is being a father.

"I think my dad and I have such a good relationship because we are so much alike, and I guess I'm that way with Jarett," Andretti said. "Jarett is a soft-spoken, soft-hearted, really good kid. He wants to do the right thing, and I want him to do the right thing. He tries especially hard, just like I did. I'm really hoping our relationship will be like the one I have with my dad."

His father also helped Andretti's mental approach.

"My dad is a perfectionist, and he wanted me to be that way too, so he pushed me that way," he said. "He lays on me pretty hard and keeps me more on my toes than I sometimes want to be, but you know, that's dads."

Aldo did have his moments in racing as well.

"My dad got to test at Indy (for the Indianapolis 500)," Andretti said. "He was running really fast. The front sway bar broke, and he spun out. He didn't hit anything, but people said he was driving over his head before they found out what happened, and he didn't get the opportunity to run.

"I was testing there on my 25th birthday. The first time I drove at Indy was awesome; we were really fast. The first time we tried to qualify we were running fast enough to qualify, and we blew an engine. The next time we went out a clamp fell off the turbo, and we were running fast enough to be the quickest that day. We had to make a third attempt, and we qualified. I was mad because I wasn't the quickest, but then I pulled in to have the pictures taken. My dad was there, and I could see in his face that I had accomplished something for both of us. That is the only time in my career that I have felt like that."

John Andretti has driven for two of NASCAR's top legends—Richard Petty and Cale Yarborough.

"They're really kind of the same," Andretti said. "They're real pleasant people to be around. They're super individuals, and they're real competitors. That's all you can really ask for. They understand the sport real well, and that makes a big difference."

In 1996, Andretti had a solid run at Daytona. Yet the fact that the win slipped away left a very bad taste in Andretti's mouth for a long time.

"Actually, it's been harder for me to deal with that than most anything else that has happened to me in stock cars, including getting hit, spinning around, crashing and hearing all the harsh words and things that have been said and written," said Andretti. "What happened to me (in 1996) at Daytona was in that pit. I understand that people are human. I guess that's how I sleep at night, with that understanding. But that's been harder for me to deal with than I thought it would be."

Andretti believes he could have—and perhaps even should have—won the race.

"I think I had a shot at it," Andretti said. "We had a real strong car. When I ran behind Terry Labonte, he had a real fast car, and Terry doesn't make any mistakes, ever, it seems like. If anybody has a perfect record, it is Terry. So, I picked him to draft with, and early in the race, we were running about eighth or ninth, and Terry was right in front of me. I said that if he'll go, no matter what happens, I'll stay with him. He pulled out, and we went to the front. Even when guys pulled out behind me, I protected Terry's spot, until Sterling Marlin finally had to do something because he had a black No. 3 jumping in and out back there who obviously wanted to lead the race pretty bad. So, Sterling got up there and led, and I kind of inherited the lead from him when he burned the motor down. We led real well from that point on. We even had to get the lead back from Ken Schrader. I missed 10 grand by about four or five feet, I think, for leading at halfway. We were just real comfortable up there. When you lead races, it's usually not that you're extending yourself because you are setting the pace. That's all we were doing, and I felt real good about that. At that point, at least until the time that we went out of the race, we had one of the cars to beat. I can't say that we would have finished the race that way, but we were a contender to that point. If it would have come down to the end, who knows? A Ford won, and Dale Jarrett wasn't right up there with us then. I don't know how much he got his car sorted out at the end. But the black No. 3 was second, and we were in front of him. We ran with them all day. Maybe experience would have cost us, who knows? We'll never know that for sure. But I think I would have known how to get the lead again."

Andretti didn't quit, and it paid off. In fact, aside from becoming a father, his win at Daytona in 1997—the first of his Winston Cup career—meant quite a bit.

"Oh, I hate to compare it, because nothing compares to when my children were born. Although the next-most exhilarating moment in my life would have to be that day at Daytona," said Andretti, who along with his wife, Nancy, has three children. "Winning races is so difficult, especially in Winston Cup. We knew we had a good shot coming in that weekend to win the race, and we may have been the only ones who knew that. To leave there with a notch on our belt is indicative of what this team is capable of and what we've done in a very short time."

Getting his first Winston Cup win put him among a small, elite group of drivers to win in the world's most prestigious racing series.

"I think there are so few winners in this series . . . You've got three guys who have won almost all the races," Andretti said. "So it's exciting to be a part of that group; it's pretty elite. It doesn't matter where you win or how you win because in Winston Cup racing there is no luck in winning much any more. Somebody can say, 'Well, he got lucky because he beat me out of the pits.' Well, he didn't get lucky; he had a better pit crew. It's so tight and so competitive that to win a race in Winston Cup means a lot. I can't imagine what it would be like to win 10 races in a season and have the potential to win more. But that's a good goal to set out there. Whether anybody else believes you can do it or not, you've got to believe in your people and yourself. This is one step toward believing that."

Andretti simply enjoys the NASCAR lifestyle, on and off the track.

"The wins and the poles are exciting...getting a pole or a win anywhere is reaching a goal," Andretti said. "There have been as many highlights off the track as on the track is what I'm saying, I guess. The fans are great, too. They're polite and they're fun to be around. I'm like everybody else, you sign your name so often, pretty soon it doesn't seem so important to sign it, but it's exciting that it's important for other people to have it. I can't sign every autograph, but the fans understand that. All those things have combined as my greatest highlights. I couldn't pick just one."

Andretti was hooked up with Cale Yarborough through a strange series of events.

"It's kind of an interesting story," Andretti said. "Tony Furr and Tony Santanicola and Bob Fisher were the key people working for Yarborough. Jeremy Mayfield was out looking for alternative employment, and they came to me in midseason and asked me to drive the car. I said, 'We can talk about that; we have some time.' They said, 'No, we want you to drive it next weekend.' I wasn't happy where I was at, so it was a good time to talk. Mayfield was negotiating with the team I was leaving, and I was talking to the one that he was leaving. So we did a late-season driver swap. I went to Cale's office; we negotiated a deal, and 10 minutes later I was driving on a handshake deal. I didn't even have a contract until February, so it was a matter of trust. I'd done that before; I drove on a handshake deal for 'The King.'"

Andretti has shunned his reputation as a driver known more for crashes than strong finishes.

"Somebody asked me one time, 'Why do you crash so much?' I

said, 'I don't crash a lot.' And he said, 'What color is the sky in your world?'" Andretti said with a laugh. "I told him that I get paid to run at the front, and I will do whatever it takes to stay there. I told the crew chief that if you give me a car that's capable of getting up front, I don't crash. And…you've seen that. If you give me a car that can do that, my fangs grow a little longer, I sit up a little straighter in the seat. If you have a 20th-place car, you're only going to get to 15th by laying everything on the line. If you can see that leader, it just does something to you and your attitude and determination."

Going from CART racing to NASCAR Winston Cup cars provided a big challenge for Andretti.

"The biggest adjustment was getting hit in the left rear quarter panel and back bumper," Andretti said in reference to the "paint swapping" and bumping in NASCAR. "In IndyCar you don't have a spotter. So you have basically two choices if you're in tight with someone: stay in there and hope something bad doesn't happen or get out of there and try again. To me, driving a race car, you have a seat, belts and a steering wheel, and you drive until you find the ragged edge; then you stay there all day long. The cars do have different feels, but I have driven so many cars that it was just another adjustment. I haven't stayed with one type of car for so long that I wasn't comfortable being in another series."

His diverse racing background has also helped.

"I have raced everything with four wheels," Andretti said. "NASCAR racing is just part of that. The thing that drew me the most to NASCAR is the level of competition. All the other series talk about competition, but nothing compares to Winston Cup. You want to be where it is the hardest to win because when you do it is such an accomplishment. It's an exciting series. I like racing a lot, and NASCAR keeps us busy. NASCAR treats your family like it is its own family. Not that the other series don't, but with a 30-plus race schedule, NASCAR makes it possible. NASCAR makes it easy off the track and difficult on it, and I like that mix."

Andretti's IndyCar background helped prepare him for the Brickyard 400. While others were making their first appearance at

Indy when NASCAR started racing at the Brickyard, Andretti was a seasoned veteran at that track.

"I have a huge advantage," Andretti said with a smile. "I know where the bathrooms are. I know where the police stake out for speeders, and I know all the back roads in, so I'd say I have an advantage."

On a serious note, Andretti does see Indy from a different perspective than many drivers.

"In a good Indy car you just go around, hold it wide open and steer," he said. "The biggest difference in a stock car is that you can drive it in too deep; you can drive it in not far enough. You've got to back off and you've got to brake at Indy. I think everyone has decided that shifting doesn't really work there because nobody does it anymore. There has been a lot of experimenting and there still is. Obviously the prize money promotes a lot of testing there. Some guys bring cars that they need to run down the straightaways. Some guys bring cars that are just killers in the corners."

Andretti has nothing but respect for the current king of the Winston Cup Series, Jeff Gordon.

"Right now, they're hitting on all 12 cylinders, and they're not missing one thing," Andretti said of the No. 24 DuPont Refinishes team. "They've got a really strong chemistry and a strong belief in one another. When they go into a race or qualifying or anything, they know they're the team to beat. That transcends through everybody, and the focus that they have transcends through everybody. There's not a lot of socializing going on there; they're just focused on that race car. But they didn't get there overnight. They're just like Dale Jarrett and Todd Parrott with the Yates team and like Jeff Burton with Roush. We've got that at Petty, but it's going to take some time.

"When you look at the 24 team, there's a lot of continuity, and that's another reason why they're so successful," Andretti said. "When you look at the list of crew chiefs in the series, there's only four that are with the same team they were with in '94, and Ray Evernham is one of them. We see all of those things from an outside point of view at Petty Enterprises, and we're getting there. I don't know if we're as talented as they are (the 24 team), but this is the best opportunity of my career to get to that level. We've still got a long ways to go, and we know it's going to take time, but I believe eventually we can get there. There's no doubt in my mind."

Andretti said the rapport and friendship between him and team owner Richard Petty, begun four years ago, is stronger than ever now.

"When you have a relationship like we had, albeit a short one, you want to keep it alive, and we did, and that's what enabled me to come back here," Andretti said. "I like being around Richard and every guy on this team. It just works. When I go to the track, there's not one thing I don't enjoy about being there. With all the demands that are put on you, there aren't many drivers out there, I think, that are as happy as I am. I like to think I have the same family values as 'The King,' and those are very strong, which is something I really admire about him."

After getting his first win at Daytona, Andretti was given a nickname by crew chief Robbie Loomis.

"Richard is 'The King,' and he'll always be 'The King' in NASCAR racing," Andretti said at the time. "Around here, they're starting to call me the 'Speedway King.' Robbie Loomis came up with that one. I can't say I totally dislike it, either. If you're a king at something, then that means you're doing something positive. That means we're headed in the right direction with our program, and we're very pleased about that. I think your first win is always pretty special because you usually have to work longer for your first one than you do for the ones thereafter. I'm hoping that's the case. Everything changes when you get to Victory Lane. I think it changes the way other drivers look at you, too."

CHAPTER 2

RICH BICKLE

Bickle's briefcase: Won back-to-back races from Bud Pole in the NASCAR Craftsman Truck Series in 1997; started 10th in NASCAR Winston Cup Series Brickyard 400 in 1997; finished second in NASCAR Craftsman Truck Series points in 1997.

Rich Bickle fell hard when it looked like he had the world at his feet coming out of the Craftsman Truck Series. And then, when it looked like he was laying at the feet of the world in 1998, he climbed on top of the world with a top-five Winston Cup finish.

Bickle's back; believe it, buddy boy—try saying that a few times fast.

Bickle, who was born May 13, 1961, started racing at age 5 in motocross and captured a 250cc crown at age 16. In the early 1980s, Bickle was more than holding his own in the upper Midwest near his hometown of Edgerton, Wisconsin, racing against such soon-to-be stars as Dick Trickle, Rusty Wallace and the late Alan Kulwicki.

Bickle made a dent in NASCAR in 1990, finishing 24th in the Daytona 500 that year. He came up with a 20th-place finish in 1992 in the Winston Cup Tyson/Holly Farms 400 at North Wilkesboro Speedway.

In 1996, Richard Petty tapped Bickle to drive a Dodge in the Craftsman Truck series. In 1997, Bickle had a breakthrough year, winning three races and taking second in the point standings to Jack Sprague.

After finishing second in the NASCAR Craftsman Truck Series points standings in 1997, Rich Bickle had big plans for the 1998 season. But when those plans fell through, Bickle was left to make do with the Busch Grand National Series.

That changed in the fall of 1998—to be more exact, on Sept. 28 at the NAPA AutoCare 500 at Martinsville.

As Ricky Rudd was courageously battling to a win for the 16th year in a row, Bickle was showing courage as well. He hadn't fared better than 18th place in the 15 races he'd run since taking over for Greg Sacks, whose season was halted because of injury.

At Martinsville, Bickle wouldn't be denied. He gutted out a fourth-place finish to show everyone that there was more certainty than uncertainty in his NASCAR future.

"I've led races that nobody could even race with me, and with 50 to go, I get a flat tire, blow up or get wrecked by a lapped car," Bickle said. "You never know what's gonna happen, and the lapped cars (at Martinsville) were scary. I mean, I think they were worse when they were coming around to get the green. They were duking for position and the 99 car (Jeff Burton) got drilled and everybody was trying to go four-wide. I just thought to myself, 'This is gonna be one of those days,' but fortunately we got track position back, and I had to fight only so many lapped cars there. It just ended up being a great day for us."

Bickle did lose the battle that day at Martinsville: fighting back tears, he emotionally thanked those who stood behind him during the tough times.

"I don't know what to say. . .it's pretty emotional for me," Bickle said as he paused to gather himself. "This is like a win. The Thorn Apple Valley Ford guys did a heckuva job. We ran out of brakes at the end. We told them (his crew) that we can run with these guys if you give me something to drive, and the guys did a heckuva job bringing me something here that was pretty danged good. I never did like this race car they had here, but even people as stubborn as I am can say that this was the best race car I drove."

Ironically, just months earlier, in April of '98, when Bickle took over the ride, car owner Cale Yarborough stated that Bickle was strong at, of all places, Martinsville, where Bickle made his initial run in the Thorn Apple Valley Ford at the Goody's Headache Powder 500.

"I think Rich is capable of getting the job done for us," team owner Yarborough said. "Rich has a lot of experience at Martinsville and is strong on the short tracks."

Of course, Yarborough was well aware that Bickle won the Hanes 250 NASCAR Craftsman Truck Series race at Martinsville in September of '97.

Although Martinsville—because of the September 1998 win—is always going to be a favorite track, Bickle likes others as well.

"There are three different ways to answer that: short tracks, road courses and superspeedways," Bickle said. "I have a favorite in each variety. But my favorite is in Wisconsin: Slinger Speedway, a track I grew up racing on. As far as superspeedways I'd have to say Charlotte; it's close to home; it's where I ran my first Cup race. As far as a road course it would have to be Watkins Glen."

Bickle actually backed into the Craftsman Truck Series.

"Back in '95, my Busch program fell apart, and I got a great offer from Richard Petty," Bickle said. "I had a couple Cup offers and some Busch offers that weren't too attractive to me, so I took the job with Richard in 1996."

The racing blood cruising through Bickle's veins runs in his family.

"My dad raced for 35 or 36 years, so I grew up around it and around the racetrack," Bickle said. "I was at the track from the time I was a month old, my mom says. My dad raced in Wisconsin for 35 years. He was a full-time construction guy during the week and a great weekend racer when he came home from work. It's something I'm very proud of."

Bickle's first Craftsman Truck win came in May 1997 in the Craftsman 200 at Portland Speedway. He had to battle Ron Hornaday for quite a while before picking up the win.

"I don't know what he's got in there for a transmission, but he gets some ungodly restarts," Bickle said of Hornaday. "We banged around a bit. I was kind of mad at him, and he was kind of mad at me. Neither one of us was going to give the other guy the groove. I was going to win this race. I knew I had the best truck…The writing was on the wall, I was going to win. To finally get one, though, is great. You know what they say, 'the first one's the hardest.' I remember it took me forever to win my first ARCA race, but then once I did, I won seven of the next 12."

Bickle still remembers that first NASCAR win. Even though he had won literally dozens of races before joining the major NASCAR series, Bickle said the first truck win was special.

"It felt like my first race, or my first short track win; it was another rung on the ladder," Bickle said. "It was very satisfying for me and everyone else involved. It was a great sense of accomplishment and a great day."

Bickle picked up his second win one week later at the NAPACARD 200 in Monroe, Washington—and made Bickle the first to pick up back-to-back wins in the NASCAR Craftsman Truck Series, quite an honor for a series that includes the likes of Hornaday, Jack Sprague and Joe Ruttman.

"To go so long without winning, then to win two straight," Bickle said, "is unbelievable. We just need to keep it going. When you've got luck on your side, you've got to ride it as long as possible."

Bickle endured a setback later that summer when he broke his ribs at the Indianapolis Motor Speedway. A flat tire caused him to crash into the wall at the Brickyard 400 Winston Cup race with only seven laps to go, but he was ready to race the following week.

"I'm ready to get back on a roll," Bickle said at the time. "This little thing isn't going to hold us down. All athletes play with pain, and this is no different. I'm sure a trip to Victory Lane will make me feel a lot better."

Not even a month later, an emergency appendectomy could have sidelined Bickle. But he came back less than two weeks later to win his third race of the season, the Hanes 250 at Martinsville Speedway.

The truck series, although under NASCAR's banner, has a unique following.

"It draws a different fan base and a different sponsor base," Bickle said. "Trucks are the No. 1-selling vehicle in the country, and people respond to that. And the sponsors have a different angle, too. An example happened in 1996: We had Georgia Pacific on our truck, and that fit. You don't go and pick up lumber in your car— you do that in your pickup truck. So I think it's a natural fit, and the popularity is to be expected."

Bickle said the truck series has a lot of talented drivers.

"All the guys that run up front are good to race with," Bickle said. "They are all champions from where they came from. That's one of the real strong points to the Craftsman Truck Series. I have raced with Jack Sprague more than any other driver in the series. Jack and I had some hellacious races at Concord. But I like running with all the guys; that's one of the reasons it's such a good series."

Driving a Busch Grand National Car and a Craftsman Truck, the biggest differences are cosmetic and under the hood.

"Trucks have a longer wheel base and more horsepower, but less downforce," Bickle said.

The Winston Cup cars and trucks have even more similarities.

"They are basically the same chassis design, except for the change to accommodate the roll bar," Bickle said. "The only thing that is different is they don't have the aerodynamic downforce that the cars have. They are similar, though."

There are also cosmetic differences within the vehicles when it comes to Winston Cup cars and the trucks.

"There is a lot of difference, probably a foot, in terms of headroom," Bickle said. "With the way the cage is built you sit more upright in the truck, and with me being 6-foot-5, it's a lot easier sitting in a truck rather than having to squish myself down to drive a Cup car. But they're both a lot of fun to drive."

Bickle's height is something that draws attention, especially since some of the sport's top drivers—such as Jeff Gordon and Mark Martin—are only 5-foot-6.

"Most drivers are real short, though I don't know why," Bickle said. "The only advantage I think they have is they carry less weight, and they sit down in the car a little better. But being built big, I think I have the ability to muscle a car later in the races; maybe I'm a little stronger after a few hours. But I don't think it's much different either way, although you're right, there are a lot more short drivers."

Over the years, Bickle has given away many of his trophies to fans.

"Back in about 1985, I started winning a lot of Late Models," Bickle said. "And through my career of winning races in motorcycles and roller skates, I had a lot of trophies and a pretty small house. So, I started looking around for kids and would just give them the trophies. I've probably given away around 200 trophies. The looks on their faces are pretty special. Especially when they'd come up to you years later and ask if you remember them. It's just a pretty neat deal."

While many drivers cite the legendary Richard Petty and Junior Johnson—among others—as their heroes, Bickle has another name that fans will know as his own role model on the track.

"Growing up back home, besides my dad, Dick Trickle was kind of my hero," Bickle said. "He's helped me out a lot over the years with advice and with equipment at times. I've raced with him for lots of years; he's kind of legend in the North short track racing. Besides that, there are a ton more guys up there that I learned from, but I'd say he's the biggest."

But don't misunderstand: Bickle has a tremendous amount of respect for Petty and continues to be grateful for their relationship.

"Richard is just a great individual," Bickle said. "When I took the deal with Richard, I knew it would be tough with the Dodge program, not having raced in years. But I knew working with him, with his experience as a driver and an owner and the way he works with people, I knew it would be beneficial to my career. It was a very good relationship, one that I will always be grateful for."

Although his plans to drive on the Winston Cup Series for Darrell Waltrip didn't happen, Bickle said driving for both Waltrip and Petty was an honor.

"They are both class acts, both great people who taught me a lot, not so much on the racetrack but off of it," Bickle said. "It's actually easier to drive for drivers, they've been behind the wheel, and they know that not everything goes perfectly every time; they know there are things that you can't control. I would say there is less pressure."

Since he's been an owner, Bickle has advice for anyone seeking to run his own team.

"If you can get people who you can trust a lot, it helps because you won't have to be doing everything yourself," Bickle said.

Crew chief/driver relationships vary. Bickle likes to, as a driver, keep himself as involved as possible.

"Basically, I've been a hands-on type of guy," Bickle said. "I think a lot of crew chiefs like that, giving them information and feedback. We'll go back-and-forth and talk about it. Most of the times I can tell the crew chief the right way to go, and we'll talk after that."

Bickle knows the key to finishing high in the race is to simply be sure to finish the race.

"I have always tried to take care of the equipment and not tear a lot of things up," Bickle said.

Bickle is proud of his Wisconsin roots and appreciates the other talent coming out of that area.

"I grew up in an era where there were so many top drivers in short track asphalt racing," Bickle said. "You'd have 40 guys out there five nights a week—great racing all over the state. I grew up with 20 of the top short track guys in the country. And you either had to get real fast or be satisfied riding around in the back, you know, just kind of make a hobby of it. I owe a lot of thanks to guys like (Dick) Trickle; they showed me a lot and taught me a lot about racing."

When he is not at the racetrack on the weekends in the fall, Bickle is watching a certain NFL team that has Wisconsin roots as deep as his own.

"I'm a big Green Bay Packers fan," Bickle said. "That's the only other sport I get into—football. I used to like to hunt and fish, but I don't have much time to do that anymore. But I think I'll pick up fishing when I retire."

Not only are Bickle's racing roots deep, so are his career roots— he has lived in and around cars almost his entire life.

"I worked for a buddy of mine that raced, working in his body shop for a couple of years," Bickle said. "I welded semitrailers back in my hometown in Wisconsin. I did other things on and off, building bodies for other people's cars, stuff that I learned from my dad. But as far as outside of racing, I've been doing this since I was only a few years old."

CHAPTER 3

BRETT BODINE

Bodine's boasts: Finished 25th in 1998 Winston Cup points standings; won the Modified Race of Champions event in 1985; was honored by the fans with the NASCAR Busch Series Grand National Division's Most Popular Driver award in 1986; finished second in 1986 NASCAR Busch Series Grand National Division championship race; first NASCAR Winston Cup Series win came in 1990 at North Wilkesboro; finished a career-best 12th in the 1990 NASCAR Winston Cup Series point standings.

Brett Bodine has racing in his blood—which is no surprise since his brothers are also among the stars of NASCAR.

With brothers Geoffrey and Todd, the Bodines are among the more well-known brothers in NASCAR history. The family's racing roots run deep.

"Our whole family got started because my grandfather and my dad were such big race fans," Bodine said. "They used to come to

Daytona and watch the beach races and travel all over to watch racing. And my grandfather wanted to turn one of his dairy farms into a dirt track. The local track wasn't treating the drivers very well, and he want to treat them better. My dad ran the track for years. All three of us got our start that way, but we never thought that all three of us would become Winston Cup drivers."

Bodine's background includes Modifieds and NASCAR Busch Series Grand National Division action where he was runner-up in 1986. Bodine was tapped to drive in place of Terry Labonte in the Junior Johnson-owned Budweiser Chevrolet in 1987 (Martinsville and North Wilkesboro). He made his NASCAR Winston Cup Series debut in the 1986 World 600 in a Rick Hendrick-owned car. He finished 17th.

Bodine's first victory came at North Wilkesboro in 1980 in his 80th start. Nineteen races later he got his first Bud Pole in the 1990 Mello Yello 500 at Charlotte.

Bodine is married. He was born January 11, 1959. The 5-7, 170-pound Bodine still lists Chemung, New York, as his hometown.

Brett and Geoffrey have been through more than their share of sibling rivalry, something that deeply splintered the family after a crash at the Brickyard that made the brothers appear to be enemies.

"Our relationship has gotten past the trouble we had after that incident at Indianapolis," Bodine said. "We're a lot closer now than we've ever been. A lot of that has to do with the passing of our father. It's been a very interesting situation, racing against my brothers. We've had great fun, and we've had family controversy, but through it all we've been able to stay a family and recognize that on the racetrack we're fierce competitors and off the racetrack we stay a close-knit family. I'm very proud of what my brothers have been able to accomplish in the sport. I think it's unbelievable that three farm boys from upstate New York have been able to make it to the top motorsports competition in the United States."

Having worn the hat of owner, Bodine knows the other side of the owner/driver relationship quite well. But he never lets it affect the way he approaches a race.

"Once I'm in the race car I don't think about being the owner," Bodine said. "I think that comes from my past, where I always treated the equipment with respect, no matter who owned it. That tends to give you a good background for owning a team. As far as owning and driving, it's hard to delegate my time between the two. I'm getting better at that, and it will make me more competitive. When I'm at the track on the weekend, I'm the driver. I don't want to hear about the problems at the shop or anything like that. I'll address those owner problems on Monday morning."

One thing Bodine has never lost sight of is the importance of family. To that end, his racing endeavors are a family affair.

"My wife and daughter go to all the races with me," Bodine said. "My daughter works with us at the race shop. We really enjoy the tracks close to home. The least amount of travel to home makes them very enjoyable. But we also really like Indianapolis and California in Fontana and Daytona because we have a condo there; it's like going to our second home."

Bodine's experience as an owner came about in legendary fashion—he bought the No. 11 team from NASCAR legend Junior Johnson. Still, even though the quality of Johnson's name is without peer, the team needed to move forward.

"When we bought the team from Junior Johnson, we kept about half the race cars and sold about half of them," Bodine said. "That's about six, and then we built six. And that's common; you're always building new cars and throwing out the ones you don't like. As far as the engines, we sold all the engine equipment that we got when we bought the team."

Todd rejoined the Winston Cup Series in 1998.

"I've always thought he's a very talented driver and deserves to be here," Bodine said of Todd. "It's unfortunate that he had to take two years off and run the Busch Series. I'm really excited about it. Todd's got a lot of potential if people will leave him alone."

Bodine cautions aspiring drivers to make well thought-out decisions before moving up in class.

"I always tell drivers competing at their local tracks that before you move up a division, make sure you're dominating the division you're in," Bodine said. "Don't move up too early because you won't win races, and you won't get the exposure. I know it's hard, but you need to be a winner in your division before you start to move up. People sometimes forget that all of us in Winston Cup were champions and winners somewhere. You just go down the list, and everyone won races somewhere. And not only the drivers, but the crew chiefs are champions from somewhere."

Bodine still thinks about his days racing back home quite often.

"I do miss the Modifieds in the Northeast, and I miss the fans," Bodine said. "I truly enjoy the Winston Cup circuit and the cars and everything that goes along with it, but I do miss the Modifieds because I have a lot of friends there that I don't get to see very often."

As a graduate of Alfred State in New York, Bodine says the value of a college education can't be overstated.

"I think it's benefited me in several ways," Bodine said. "I majored in mechanical engineering, and that helped me early in my career when I had to build and maintain all my own equipment. That still applies today in understanding what it takes to make these Winston Cup cars handle. Also, just going to college, no matter what you study, helps you learn how to solve problems. It helps you mature and become a better person. It helped me understand and handle the responsibilities of being a driver today; it's not just driving the car but representing your sponsor well. I think Alfred helped me in many ways."

Although Bodine had plenty of possible investments outside of starting a team, he couldn't pass up the chance.

"Maybe people might ask, why own a race team? Why do that rather than make good money driving cars and then investing in car dealerships or restaurants, which seems to be the fashionable thing to do now?" Bodine said. "This is what I love. All of this—the sport, the people, everything. It's tough. Winston Cup racing is particularly tough. But it is what I want to do and love to do."

The new title was nothing compared to all the responsibilities.

"The biggest difference (being an owner) is that I have a finger on all aspects of the operation," Bodine said. "I'm totally involved in every facet: budgeting, scheduling, management and operations. As a driver, my main channel of communication was with my crew chief and discussing car set-up, strategy or design. But now, away from the track, I have got to focus on the things that will help keep this business operating effectively. It's a very diverse role, but one I have worked long and hard to obtain."

Of course, Brett and his wife, Diane, didn't make a rash decision to own a team.

"Diane and I were extremely prepared when we started this whole endeavor," Bodine said. "We did our homework, and nothing came as a surprise because I've been involved with the sport in so many ways throughout my career. Diane and I have always dreamed of owning our very own Winston Cup race team. Even when I was racing Modifieds, our ultimate goal was to end up in Winston Cup and eventually call all the shots."

The growth of NASCAR's popularity has forced the elimination of races at some smaller tracks while adding races at new venues in other geographic regions.

"I think our sport is going to continue to grow, and we have to make sure it does so in the appropriate way," Bodine said. "I'm not saying it's right or necessary that we lose racetracks like North Wilkesboro. We have to remember where the sport came from and what those racetracks still have to offer—a very competitive race in a different environment than a superspeedway environment. We, as a racing fraternity, need to make sure we don't overlook the value of such racetracks like North Wilkesboro and Martinsville. Racing at the short tracks helps us keep in touch with the fans because of the competitiveness of the racing and the closeness of the fans to the racing.

"One of my favorite racetracks is Martinsville Speedway. Whenever you've had a lot of success at a particular track, you can't help having it be one of your favorites. From early in my career as a full-time NASCAR Modified driver through my Busch Grand National career and into Winston Cup, I've been very fortunate to be very competitive at Martinsville. Thus, every time we go there, we're a little more confident than at some other racetrack."

Ironically, Bodine's first big NASCAR opportunity came at Martinsville.

"Probably my biggest break came from Rick Hendrick when he asked me to substitute drive for Geoffrey in a Busch Grand National race at Martinsville," Bodine said. "That was a big break for me in my career. Then to go out and win that race was really the jump-start my career needed in the eyes of the car owners in the Grand National and Winston Cup division. The transition from Modified racing in the Northeast to Busch Grand National racing in the South wasn't as difficult as I had anticipated. But the transition from Busch Grand National into Winston Cup was much harder than I anticipated. And I think we continue to see that today with other people's careers who make the move into Winston Cup."

NASCAR has grown the right way, Bodine said.

"I think and feel very strongly that NASCAR will continue to grow throughout the U.S.," Bodine said. "You will see continued expansion of the Winston Cup series in parts of the country we're not in yet. This expansion will be critical to the continued attraction of corporate America into our sport."

The 1997 season went south when sponsorship concerns left Brett pondering his future. But with a new sponsor in 1998, the potential was back. Still, Bodine doesn't enjoy the memories of 1997, when they lost their sponsor. "The very trying year we had is one thing nobody should have to go through," Bodine said. "We didn't do anything that led to the sponsor going away. We put everything we had on the line to get this team, and it wasn't fair for something like that to happen. I bought the team for a lot of reasons. You can drive a race car all your life, but you've got to do something to prepare for later."

His favorite driver as a child? Easy, No. 43—The King.

"Richard Petty was always my guy. I liked his color of cars when I was a kid," Bodine said. "He was such a friendly person."

CHAPTER 4

GEOFFREY BODINE

Geoffrey's best: Finished 27th in 1998 Winston Cup points standings; first career NASCAR Winston Cup Series win at Martinsville in spring of 1984 in his 69th career start; won the 1986 Daytona 500 on his way to an eighth-place finish in the final NASCAR Winston Cup Series standings; won the title in the 1987 International Race of Champions (IROC) Series; raced to Victory Lane at the 1996 Bud at the Glen at Watkins Glen, N.Y., for his first win since 1994; 55 Modified wins in one season is still listed in Guinness Book of World Records; won first race as a car owner in 1996 Bud at the Glen.

Bodine was born on April 18, 1949, in the family's long-time roots of Chemung, New York. He has two sons, Matthew and Barry.

The Bodine brothers—Geoffrey, Todd and Brett—are among the most recognized trio of siblings in the sport. From time to time, Geoffrey, Todd and Brett kick around the idea of combining their talents into one three-car team.

"It will take quite a bit to get us all in one operation," Bodine said. "But it's possible."

And Bodine does check in with his brothers when the schedule allows them to be racing at the same venue.

"Brett and I discuss things from time to time, or Brett's crew chief and my crew chief will discuss setups and conditions at the track," Bodine said. "So the answer is, sometimes. We don't park side by side in the garage—we have, but normally we are separated by other cars. Things happen so fast during practice and after qualifying in preparation for the race that we don't always have time to discuss things. We might after, but during it's very hard to do it at that time. With Todd being in Busch Grand National, we are separated by different garage areas, sometimes different tracks. So our communication is limited at times, but we'll go out to dinner and talk about things we've tried and what has worked and hasn't worked. So I guess the answer is yes, sometimes we do discuss those things. With Todd, we probably talk more about our horses. He and Lynn have horses, and I have a horse. We talk about our horses, and we talk about family things and things other than racing when we are together. Plus, Todd and I talk about our Harleys. So it's a mix."

During one weekend in particular, Bodine had a hard time qualifying for a race because Todd and Brett had been through a tough time, and Bodine felt like another problem might be hard on their mother.

"We were running very good Friday in practice, even after Todd crashed," Bodine said. "Then we were sitting there in line set to qualify and Brett was just in front of me. And he crashed. His crash, along with Todd's crash, slowed me down a little bit. It was my mother's birthday. And I knew when she found out that Todd and Brett crashed, it would be hard on her. If I had crashed too, she couldn't have handled that. So all I thought about was 'don't crash.' I was only thinking about surviving the day."

The consistent winners draw a lot of attention from the media, but also from the drivers not riding among the top 10 or so.

"I envy the way Mark Martin and Jeff Gordon have been

running this year and winning," Bodine said during the 1998 season. "It makes my team and me more motivated to work harder and try to go out there and compete and win. When that win does come, believe me, it will feel really good. And we feel like that win is close by. We've had a very good car the last several races; we just haven't had the good racing luck to go with our good car. We feel like when we get some good racing luck, we'll have an excellent chance of running up front and hopefully winning."

While he entered the 1998 off-season without a ride, Bodine was certain he would return to the track soon.

"I'm not exactly certain how long I'll keep driving," Bodine said. "Right now, I'm very motivated and excited about driving. I want to race; I love racing and don't think about retiring at all. But when I do, and I know I'll have to one day, I hope to stay involved in racing in some capacity. I definitely plan on helping my son, Barry. I don't know if I'll be a team owner or just a team adviser and consultant. I'll have to wait and see what I do when it happens."

Bodine finished the 1997 season without a victory for the second time in three years, but he did put together five straight finishes of 12th or better in late summer and rode that momentum to a respectable 22nd-place finish in the NASCAR Winston Cup Series standings.

Bodine was the original member of an effort that has evolved into the Rick Hendrick stable of three teams. After winning the NASCAR Rookie of the Year title in 1982, Bodine became the driver for the All-Star Racing effort owned by Hendrick at the beginning of the 1984 season, working with veteran crew chief Harry Hyde. By the time the first season was over, Bodine had notched three victories and a like number of poles. His racing resumé includes the 1986 Daytona 500 win and the International Race of Champions title in 1987.

Bodine actually got his entree to NASCAR Winston Cup Series racing by winning a NASCAR Busch Series Grand National Division race at Darlington, and he learned his tricks from none other than David Pearson, Darlington's all-time victories leader.

"In 1982, I came to Darlington for the first time to run a Late Model race," Bodine said. "I figured it would be pretty smart to follow someone who knew how to get around the track, and David Pearson was the best at Darlington. So I ended up following David around, and he showed me how to drive that track. He taught me that day to race the track and not the competition, until you have to. He didn't know he was teaching me anything. There was no verbal communication between us—I just followed him around all day. But he was a pretty good teacher because I ended up beating him and everyone else that day."

In 1994, Bodine won the Winston Select, NASCAR's all-star event at Charlotte Motor Speedway, along with the Bud Pole Award, for winning the most pole positions during the season. Bodine was the NASCAR Winston Cup Series Rookie of the Year in 1982. He won his first pole that year, at the Firecracker 400 in Daytona. His first career win came in his 69th start, at Martinsville in the spring of 1984. He has an IROC title to his credit, claimed in 1987, and a career-best NASCAR Winston Cup Series championship finish of third, in 1990.

While Bodine didn't finish in the top 20 for points in 1998, he has been in the top 10 several times. He has 18 career victories in Winston Cup and 37 Bud Poles.

Being an owner was something Bodine simply found overbearing at times.

"Owning a team can be very distracting for a driver," Bodine said. "A driver/owner needs good support people helping him manage and run a team. But a good owner/driver or a good athlete should be able to separate the ownership from the driving when he's behind the steering wheel. He can't afford to worry about the ownership part when he's racing."

While many folks fretted over Ford phasing out the Thunderbird, Bodine said the Taurus' results did the talking—Ford was, by far, the dominant car of the 1998 Winston Cup season.

"The Taurus has proven itself this year to be a great race car,"

Bodine said. "There's absolutely no chance that I know of in the near future of Ford or the Ford race teams using a T-Bird body.

"The Taurus is a great car. It's so great that NASCAR took some spoiler from us," Bodine said. "Compared to the T-bird, which was an awesome race car in its day, the Taurus is better; it has better aerodynamic balance. It drives better in traffic, especially at the bigger tracks. And even though we have less spoiler, it's still out there winning races. Ford has a lot of good teams out there running the Taurus."

Many drivers have a favorite track. Bodine likes all the tracks primarily for the inherent qualities that make each unique.

"I really don't have a favorite racetrack," Bodine said. "I think the different tracks, the variety of tracks from road courses, short tracks, medium-sized tracks to superspeedways, is part of what makes NASCAR so exciting for the race fans to watch and for the drivers, like myself, to participate in. Because I like all types of racetracks, the variety is fun."

Bodine is an accomplished driver on road courses—he won the Bud at the Glen (Watkins Glen) in 1996.

"I always love going back to Watkins Glen, and I love road racing," Bodine said. "I hope it's obvious. We've won at Riverside (Calif.), Sears Point and Watkins Glen."

Although the superspeedways are getting a lot of attention because of the restrictor plates, and the road courses get attention because they are more than just "turn left, turn left" racing, Bodine remains a fan of the short tracks.

"We need to always have short tracks—I love 'em," Bodine said. "If I were to build a racetrack right now, I'd build a short track. I'd build a short track with the highest grandstand I could find, all the way around."

In 1997, Bodine was amazed to see how the California Speedway had taken shape.

"I was there two years ago, and all I saw were the ruins of the factories," said Bodine about the site, formerly a Kaiser Aluminum manufacturing facility. "When I flew in, I looked down and saw the track. I thought, 'It can't be; it must be something else. . .' It was amazing what it had transformed into. The entrance looks like you're going into Disney World, with palm trees and landscaping. All the parking areas are paved."

The new venues present a challenge to NASCAR: Expansion to new areas and tracks brings more revenue, but some fans want to see the traditional tracks keep their spots in the series.

"We don't want to lose any of the tracks we're running at now," Bodine said. "But bringing in new tracks in new markets that are gonna pay a lot of money is good for the sport.

"I love road racing," Bodine said. "We need all the ovals we have but a couple more road races would be nice. It's pretty cool."

One thing Bodine is certain of is that the driver/crew chief relationship must click at every turn.

"Experience is what a driver feeds off of to make the right adjustments to his car," Bodine said. "A good crew chief helps with his knowledge and experience. Having experience in their background is crucial for the driver and the crew chief to make the right adjustments through the course of a race. Things change so dramatically through the course of a race that their experience can either win a race or lose a race for them."

One thing Bodine likes to do is ride his Harley, and he stays involved in his buddy Kyle Petty's charity ride. Bodine also loves the outdoors.

"I've said this many times: If anybody has any spare time, spend it in the United States," Bodine said. "This is the most beautiful country in the whole world."

Bodine hasn't forgotten his racing roots, which extend all the way to Chemung Speedrome where he received guidance from a special veteran driver.

"Herbie Green—that goes back to the first years I raced at Chemung," Bodine said. "He was kind of like a mentor; he was a really tough racer. He, along with several others there, really showed me how to race, how to drive and how to compete. Those are the kinds of things that I remember a lot because without that kind of education from guys like Herbie Green, I might not be the racer I am today."

Bodine is big on education and is proud that he has something to fall back on.

"I'm glad I'm doing this," Bodine said. "I realize how lucky I am to do something for a living that I really enjoy. I went to college and studied engineering. And I was in the military for a while, so I probably could make a living doing something else. I don't know what it'd be, but I'm glad I could do it this way, driving race cars."

Barry Bodine, Geoffrey's son, is a driver to watch for in the near future.

"He's definitely showing a lot of talent," Bodine said.

While most fans might think Winston Cup drivers fly around town before and after races, Bodine claims the opposite is more the standard.

"Driving a street car after being in a Winston Cup race at 200 mph does seem pretty slow," Bodine said. "But, believe it or not, most of us drivers do obey speed limits. And, actually, we're probably more safe than most because we realize the differences between a NASCAR Winston Cup race car and my Lincoln Mark VIII that I drive on the highway. Race cars are made for crashing; they can fly through the air at 200 mph and survive. In a street car crash at 40 mph you can die. So I'm very careful, even after a high-speed race at Talladega where we're going 200 mph."

Bodine has felt the effects of restrictor-plate racing firsthand, going from not racing at Talladega to finishing in the top 10 at California in a two-week span in 1998.

"The race at Talladega, the restrictor-plate races, especially the qualifying, are kind of out of the driver's control," Bodine said. "You just push the gas to the floor and hope it goes fast enough for the race. As a driver, you can't do anything to get it to go any faster. But at California, and all of our other tracks, you can. We don't have restrictor plates. In other words, the driver has to drive the car, and if he drives the car better than the competition, he'll do better.

Restrictor-plate racing is very frustrating for drivers because we know so little of it is skill. In a race, skill is important, especially for not causing wrecks. So, not qualifying at Talladega was very disappointing, but my team, my partners and I are fixing that. When we went to California, however, we knew we had as much of a chance as anyone else. We knew we could qualify well and race well, which we did."

Racing under green is great for speed, but drivers do assume there will be cautions at some point in a race. When the race is almost caution-free, it can throw a wrench into pitting plans.

"It really does," Bodine said. "We normally count on some cautions, if we're behind, to group everyone back up. And the cautions give us a little more time to make adjustments to a car, and the chassis, if it isn't quite right. Plus, cautions eliminate some competition, and that's an easy way to gain position. But a caution-free race normally stretches the field out because on the green flag pit stops some drivers get in and out faster than others. One second at a place like Talladega is approximately the length of a football field when you get up to speed. So it places a lot of importance on the crew in a race like that. Without a doubt, a caution-free race spreads the field out tremendously and really makes it a pretty boring race."

Having experience as a car owner, Bodine makes sure not to overburden himself so he can keep his concentration on driving.

"It can take away a focus on driving if you let it," Bodine said. "It can be very, very time consuming dealing with all the things it takes to run a race team. People, organizing, the work being done, each person's responsibilities, making sure bills are paid, insurance, on and on and on, all the things that it takes to run a business."

The frustration of not finishing high for a few years took a toll on Bodine, who nonetheless continued to push forward.

"Sometimes it isn't easy, but I've been in this business for a long while," Bodine said. "And you have to understand that you are going to have some good days and some bad days. That's why I appreciate the good days when they happen. Everything has been explainable, but that's how we deal with it. If you can't explain it, it can be frustrating, but if you can, then you deal with it."

While Winston Cup—and all other NASCAR—drivers are busy year-round, Bodine has an interesting side hobby, one that he takes very seriously.

"I got involved in bobsledding by going for a ride in one and learning that the one I was in, and the ones the Olympic athletes used, weren't American-made," Bodine said. "And being a proud American, I thought that was totally unacceptable. So, I decided to build them. We supply bobsleds for athletes at no charge, and we supply a mechanic to maintain and work on them for no charge. We're going to continue this as long as we can, with support from sponsors and the public."

Being involved in NASCAR requires Bodine to constantly stay on his toes, leaving little time for off-season interests. "We really don't have much of an off-season," Bodine said. "We end in November and start racing again in February. In January we are testing. So I consider December our offseason. I like to ski a little bit, but we have our NASCAR banquet in December, so there are a lot of things going on in December still connected with racing. There is the Drivers' Wives Auxiliary Cruise, to benefit charity. I haven't been yet, but it sounds like fun; maybe I'll go this year. So there are a lot of other things, but we do try to take a little time off for ourselves. Some drivers take more than others. My son Barry and I would like to go skiing this year; maybe some of you skiers will see us out there this December. I'm the guy going really slow," he said with a laugh. "We try to do a few things to unwind. And I can only speak for myself, but by the time Christmas comes around, I'm ready to go racing. I miss it, myself."

Bodine's crew chief for a while on the No. 7 Ford was Tim Brewer, who worked long hours with NASCAR legend Junior Johnson.

"Geoffrey's an excellent race car driver—he's won on speedways, short tracks, intermediate tracks, and he's a really good road course racer," Brewer said. "We were together with Junior Johnson, and we did real well together, I think we were third in 1990. We didn't do as well the next year, but he came back to win some races and win some poles."

Bodine knows that to succeed in the Winston Cup Series, he will have to, perhaps for his next ride, look at joining a multi-car team if he wants to finish among the top 10 in the points standings.

"We all see the advantages of the multi-car teams in NASCAR," Bodine said. "There are a number of ways of sharing information that can help each team. Plus, in some races, team cars can help each other. We need to take advantage of all that. And the way you do that is either start another team or partner up with a team that's already out there."

At Talladega in 1998, Bodine picked up his 500th career start. It's a mark he treasures, but for an all-time high, he points to the very fact that he is involved with NASCAR at all.

"I have several very, very proud moments that I could mention in my career," Bodine said. "Winston Cup racing has been my life for a long time, and that is what I wanted when I moved south in the late '70s. As busy as we are nowadays, you don't have many opportunities to reflect on your accomplishments. But just getting to race in NASCAR and Winston Cup is an accomplishment that I didn't know would happen. It was just a dream I had many years ago. . ."

CHAPTER 5

WARD BURTON

Burton's baubles: Finished 16th in 1998 Winston Cup points standings; first career NASCAR Winston Cup victory came at Rockingham in 1995; finished in top seven in three of final four races in 1995.

In 1997, Ward Burton finished 34th or lower eight times, including a streak of five early in the year. However, he also sped to seven top-10 finishes that year—his third full season in the No. 22 Pontiac—as he finished 24th in the standings.

In October of 1998, Burton came up with a second-place finish behind Mark Martin at the Charlotte Motor Speedway in the UAW-GM 500. Still, it has been three years since Burton's only Winston Cup win—which came in the ACDelco 400 at the North Carolina Speedway in Rockingham in 1995. More importantly, the second place to Martin was Burton's first top five in 85 races, dating back to 1995.

"All I know is that the guys (his crew) did a heck of a job today," said Burton, who is from South Boston, Virginia. "All the guys worked really hard. My hat's off to them. I'm really excited about this. We haven't had what we've wanted to have the last couple of years, but we can see the light at the end of the tunnel. I'm pumped."

The week before the second-place, Burton was 11th at Martinsville. Before that, his best finishes were a pair of eighth-places, at Talladega in April and in June at Michigan.

The Bill Davis Racing Team had made several changes before the race, including the changing of the crew chief with the hiring of Tom Baldwin Jr.

"A lot of stuff is changing," said Burton. "You probably can't see it. A lot of things are happening. Bill (Davis) has done a good job."

Davis said the second-place showed that the No. 22 team was on the right track.

"We made some steps we've been needing to make for a long time," Davis said. "I don't think anybody can really deny that, but we hadn't done it; we hadn't closed the deal. Today, we closed the deal. Potential turned into performance today. Instead of running half the race like that, we ran the whole race. We had great pit stops today. The motor was awesome. Nobody has more motor than we do."

Burton, who started 13th, led the race from lap 91 to lap 125 before Ernie Irvan passed him.

"I was a little bit loose all day," said Burton, who was born Oct. 25, 1961. "I know I had him (Mark Martin) beat on motor; there's no doubt about that. My guys have got some awesome motors. We were just off on chassis a little bit. He (Martin) was beating me down in three and four, and I could gain back and was equal to him in one and two. He just had a little bit on me in three and four. All my MBNA team is just working real good together right now. We beat everybody but one car, and I wanted that one car awful bad, but that's a good start."

Burton said the frustrating part was that Martin was simply on fire.

"But right now, I'm really proud because of what this team accomplished (in finishing second)," Burton said. "The chemistry is great and the guys are working hard. We're building momentum for next year."

Like a lot of others, Burton began racing early. He drove go-karts starting when he was 8 years old. Later, he was behind the wheel in Street Stock and Late Model Stocks on Virginia short tracks, primarily at his home track of South Boston Speedway where he was voted Most Popular Driver there in 1989.

Burton moved on to the NASCAR Busch Grand National series in 1990, where he finished behind his younger brother, Jeff, for Rookie of the Year.

Burton is a graduate of the Hargrove Military Academy where he was the top-ranked shooter on the school rifle team.

The "drive" to improve is one of the things that keeps Burton going.

"Personally, I think a driver, or anybody in professional sports, is looking to be better," Burton said. "I've worked real hard to get better physically and also to be more positive. And that's something that's hard to do sometimes. Those are two things that we work on all the time."

Burton is also close to Dave Blaney, who is among the rising talents within NASCAR.

"I've spent quite a bit of time with him at the track," said Burton, who lists his heroes as his father, John Burton, and driving legend Bobby Allison. "Blaney's a talented racer. He's had more bad luck than he's deserved, and I try to keep him pumped up and not get too down. We talk about a few things, about certain tracks. So, you know, we talk quite often."

Burton has also been able to "work" with Jeff off the track—on the television. It is something he wouldn't mind doing more of in the future.

"That's something that Exide and those other sponsors have to decide," Burton said. "Ever since we did our first commercial of us walking down pit lane at Daytona, the president of Exide really liked that. It's been fun. I like doing television commercials and I hope to do more. I don't know the format of the next one, but from what I know, there will be another one. I think everyone liked the last one we did at the NASCAR Cafe in Nashville."

At Talladega, Burton tangled with Dale Earnhardt and Bill Elliott. He knew he had to talk to the two respected drivers since Burton was responsible for the accident.

"When I got home from the race, I called Richard Childress because he was the only one whose number I knew," Burton said. "The next day I tried to contact Dale, and he returned my phone call, but I was out. Bill was really nice to me; he said he was OK and just sore. He said he'd been on both sides of the coin. And Dale, by returning the phone call, was a real gentleman. I looked up to both of them before, and I do even more now. They're both really good people, and I appreciate them approaching me the way they did and making me feel better about it."

Owning up to his responsibility is just part of being a driver.

"I'm a lot of things in life, but dishonest is not one of them," Burton said. "I could see that I had made a little mistake and caused big problems for the other drivers, my fellow competitors. It really soured my whole day, my whole week."

Burton was able to learn from his father about the joy of racing.

"I got started at an early age with the enthusiasm my dad had for speed," Burton said. "From there I went to a military school and college, and it was a long time before I was back in racing. The biggest thing I have to attribute to my success is that I have had a lot of people help me. My family has helped a lot."

Burton said the things that have made him successful are the same that lead to good things off the track.

"The biggest advice for young drivers is that you work hard, and whatever you do, you do it 100 percent," Burton said. "I didn't have a lot of direction in my life. But that first time I was in a car, that was it. So you've just got to get a goal and give it 100 percent."

When Burton gets away from the track, he gets WAY away, getting in touch with nature.

"My hunting activities have changed because of my wildlife conservation habits," Burton said. "Conservation, in my mind, is No. 1. I've really started to enjoy going elk hunting in places like Canada and Montana. Just being in those areas is great."

Burton looks forward to joining a bigger team in the future.

"We share a little bit of information with Petty Enterprises, the 43 and 44. It's probably not enough," Burton said. "By having a single-car owner, I don't get as much information as those big teams. For every lap I run, I get one lap of information, while they each get two, three or more laps of information. It's tough."

After spending a day a week in the racing shop—usually Tuesday—Burton tries to involve his family in his career.

"My family goes to probably half to three-quarters (of the races)," said Burton, who likes spending time at home with his wife, Tabitha, and their children. "My wife goes a little more often than the kids because she's always worried something is going to happen to me. We have a motor home that allows us to stay together. About half the drivers have those. But one thing that's really helped is Motor Racing Outreach; they've done a great job promoting a family atmosphere at the racetrack."

Don't be surprised to see Burton turning up—like his brother Jeff—in Busch Grand National races in the future.

"It's turning into a thing that when you run on Saturday, you can learn a lot for Sunday," he said. "I helped a guy out at Texas in qualifying, but there's still a big difference in speed and power."

Burton had plenty of success qualifying during the 1998 season but seemed to be farther back in the pack at the finish line. It is something he is well aware of.

"They've given me some great cars for qualifying," Burton said. "We need to work on our race package, particularly from mid-race to the end of the race. We've had some deals where maybe some of the calls I've made from the driver's seat haven't been right. We've had some engines lose their steam later in a race. Overall, our communication skills need improving. We need to make sure that when I make a call about what the race car is doing, we know what to do about it."

In July of 1997, Burton suffered a concussion and bruised ribs from a last-lap wreck while he was running in the top five in the Pepsi 400 at Daytona.

"I tell you, that's the hardest I've ever hit, and I daggum sure don't want to do it again," Burton said. "I had never had bruised ribs before, so I didn't know if I had stomach problems or not. I couldn't sit up in the hospital. They X-rayed my stomach and all that, and come to find out it was my ribs, specifically my floating ribs, down the very bottom at the side of the rib cage. They were really bruised. My neck was stretched, and I had a bump on the forehead because of the helmet hitting the steering wheel. All in all, the seat in the car and the belts, everything did like it was supposed to. It was just a terrific impact. I've never even come close to hitting anything so hard before."

Ward Burton posted a lap of 181.561 miles an hour to win his first Bud Pole of the '98 season for the Miller Lite 400 at Michigan Speedway in mid-June of '98.

The line between "competitive" team and "contending" team is fine, but there's no doubt when a team has crossed into the elite category.

"It's not magic," Burton said. "But there are certain ingredients that every team is looking for. When you've got it, it feels like magic. When you don't, you definitely know you don't have it. Some of us don't get it consistently enough to run where we want to run every week. The 22 team is representative of many teams in the Winston Cup garage—hardworking, hopeful. They could be, maybe should be, at the front of the field."

The demands of coordination, strength, communication and—in many cases—working with a teammate or teammates are what make NASCAR one of the toughest things for an athlete to succeed at.

"This is the toughest sport of racing automobiles in the world," Burton said. "You just have to stay focused and address things as you get to them."

CHAPTER 6

DALE EARNHARDT

Earnhardt's effort: Winner of seven NASCAR Winston Cup titles; missed his eighth (and third consecutive) by 34 points in 1995; has won more money than any other driver in history of racing, worldwide; finished eighth in 1998 Winston Cup points standings; has won every major event and title available to NASCAR Winston Cup drivers; triumphed at Indianapolis Motor Speedway in 1995 (one of his five wins), putting his name into the record books at the famed track.

His eyes have the stare of a convict on death row. And if you had to ask any driver who he would least like to have on his bumper for the last lap of a race, Dale Earnhardt would be near the top.

The Intimidator. Black car, No. 3 on the side. Of course, if you want to know about Dale Earnhardt, start with this: His favorite movie? "Cool Hand Luke."

He is amazing on the track, and his fan following off the track is just as incredible. His legend is as cemented as possible.

He's even overcome various struggles. In 1997, for the first time since 1981, Earnhardt was unable to win a race, and his fifth-place points finish was his lowest since 1992. However, that just shows how strong the No. 3 team has been over the years. Their "down year" would be a dream season for the vast majority of competitors on the NASCAR Winston Cup Series.

Things definitely seemed to be coming around for Earnhardt late in 1997. He posted four top-fives and six top-10s in the last eight races, leading many to believe that a return to Victory Lane was just around the corner, which couldn't have been more true since he opened with the big, long-awaited win at Daytona.

"It's neat being paid for what you enjoy doing," said Earnhardt, who was born April 29, 1951. "I'm not ready to quit, and I'm not sure I will be at the end of the contract. As guys get older, they get smarter, and they don't forget the things they have done. I don't. Everything has gotten better. When I sit down in a race car, it's like the first day I ever raced. There is nothing else on my mind. I'm focused on driving that car and on beating the guy in front of me and beating the guy on my bumper."

Earnhardt's seven NASCAR Winston Cup Series titles offer all the proof needed to those who question his place in history. His aggressive style has helped define a generation of drivers, those who run hard on Sunday, then shake hands and exchange congratulations when all is said and done.

Earnhardt was the first driver in the history of the sport to win the Rookie of the Year Award and the series title at the NASCAR Winston Cup level. He was the first three-time winner of the Winston Select (1987, '90 and '93), and he has won two IROC championships (1990 and '95).

"I had a long dry spell, and sometimes that was hard to live with," he said. "Then I won the Daytona 500, and that was great. And that eighth championship will happen, too."

Earnhardt and Richard Petty each have won seven NASCAR Winston Cup titles.

"It's about winning," he said. "I couldn't tell you how much it pays to win the race at Martinsville. The money is an incentive, but if it didn't pay anything, I would still want to win. I want to win every race. That's what it's all about. If you're not competitive for the win, you're not going to win the championship. Today, it takes those top-five finishes and consistent runs and a win or two to win the championship."

Earnhardt credits Rod Osterlund with giving him his biggest break in 1978. He won the championship for Osterlund, his first, in 1980 before moving on to drive for Richard Childress, for whom he has won six titles.

Earnhardt owns a farm in Mooresville, North Carolina, where he has horses, dogs, cats, bulls and chickens. He owns a 76-foot Hatteras boat, bass boat, a Lear Jet 31A with two full-time pilots, and a KingAir 200.

"Having the Intimidator as a boss is a lot different than I thought it would be," said veteran NASCAR crew chief Philippe Lopez, who joined Earnhardt's DEI group. "I was under the same impression as everyone else, but once I've met him, he's just a super guy. And he's the best boss I've had yet."

When Dale Earnhardt and Terry Labonte took the green flag for the MBNA Gold 400 at Dover Downs International Speedway in September of 1998, it marked the 600th start for Earnhardt.

"It sneaks up on you," Earnhardt said. "You go from track to track and season to season just thinking about racing and not really looking at the numbers. Then one day they tell you you're about to reach 600 starts, and you realize it is a pretty big accomplishment. There haven't been many drivers that have reached this plateau. Four out of the top 10 are still racing today. I think that says a lot for NASCAR and its safety programs. The drivers are able to compete week in and week out and avoid injuries. The sport has changed tremendously over the years, and the competition is the best it's ever been. Each week the field gets closer and closer when it comes to qualifying. When we started this tour 20 years ago, there were a couple of seconds between first and 40th; now it's down to hundredths of a second."

One of his biggest fans runs RCR—Richard Childress Racing.

"I knew I wanted him to drive my car the first time I saw him drive somebody else's," Earnhardt's car owner and long-time friend Richard Childress said. "His desire and sheer determination to be the best at what he does is amazing. I've always thought he was the best, even when I raced against him. I've been fortunate to be a big part of Dale's career. Together I think we've accomplished more than either of us ever could have imagined. It's been 15 years, six championships and many trips to Victory Lane. I'm proud to be associated with him professionally, but even prouder to call him my friend."

The legend of Earnhardt is one that it is quite unique.

"There's Earnhardt and then there's everybody else," says Bud Moore, for whom Earnhardt drove in 1982 and '83 and who has fielded cars at one time or another for 12 different drivers. "The biggest thing about Earnhardt is his desire. When he slides down in that race car, he is going to go to the front if it's at all possible. He'll find a way to get there. He's looking up ahead all the time, figuring out his next move. When he goes into a turn, he knows what he's going to do when he gets there. He's going to go high or he's going to go low, but he knows. He doesn't get there and then say, 'What do I do now?' Talent is talent, then or now. And he's got the talent."

All of the other legends in the sport mean a lot to Earnhardt.

"Shoot, in the beginning, you just wanted to race. That's what you wanted to do, and you wanted it so bad that was all you worked for. You didn't think about what you're going to accomplish or what you could accomplish, you just wanted to race," Earnhardt said. "You go to the race and you see other guys race, the Pettys and Pearsons and Allisons and Yarboroughs, and then you get the opportunity to be in the same race with them one day and that's just astounding to you. That's the way it was with me."

Earnhardt is amazed only by the fact that he's allowed to race for living. He was almost overwhelmed when he was named one of the top drivers of all time in NASCAR.

"A racer wants to race and win," Earnhardt said. "Imagine having the opportunity to do that for a living, and then to be successful, and then to be considered one of the greatest drivers that ever raced—especially by a group of peers—is one of the greatest honors a driver could ever receive."

That desire to win is still strong.

"I want to do the best I can every race," Earnhardt said. "I don't like it when I don't. When I sit down in that race car, that's it. There's nothing else on my mind. There are a bunch of guys heading for the finish line, and I want to get there first. I want to win. The will to win hasn't diminished. There's one thing on my mind when a race starts: How am I going to get to the front?"

Earnhardt had a horrific crash at Talladega in 1996, suffering a broken left clavicle and sternum.

"When the car turned abruptly sideways, I knew I was going to hit the wall," Earnhardt said. "When I hit the wall I broke my sternum. When the car got up on its side and in the air a little bit, it was spinning around, and I saw a flash. Another car hit me at the same time, so it was probably Derrike (Cope). Then there was a big crash and the car went airborne again and that's when I broke my collarbone and bruised my pelvis. That was when the No. 3 car hit me. And then the car sat back down on its wheels and spun around. The No. 29 car went by to my left, and then a red car hit the front end. The car stopped. The smoke was rolling out from under the dash because the wires were burning because the dash was knocked down in the car so far from the top collision. I switched the battery switch off. I started trying to unbuckle my helmet. I knew my collarbone was hurt. At about the same time, the safety crews and NASCAR's Steve Peterson and Buster Auten got to me. Like I told 'em, 'Don't cut the top off; I think I can get out.' So they worked with me and pulled me out of the car. And then I tried to. . . well, I wanted to lay down. I didn't want to stand up. But I couldn't because it hurt too bad starting to lay down. My chest hurt too bad, so I said, 'Just walk me to the ambulance.' That's why I was walking instead of laying on the stretcher."

While many would point to that crash as an example of NASCAR's dangers, Earnhardt believes just the opposite.

"I think being in good shape is a plus for anything," Earnhardt said. "I'm telling you, I feel safe in our race cars; I feel safe in the seats and the harnesses and the sensing equipment I use, and the open-face helmet. If I'd had a full-face helmet, I think I would have hurt my neck. And I have no neck injuries. I held on to the steering wheel completely the whole time. I was bouncing around in the car, but I was still braced in there pretty good. I was comfortable with that, and I don't have any second thoughts or I wish I had this or I wish I had that. I think I had the safest everything in the car and a safe race car when it was all over. When you walk away from that, it's a pretty good testimony to your physical fitness and the safety of your race car and the equipment you use."

Still, Earnhardt couldn't wait to get behind the wheel the week after the crash.

"I reckon it's sorta like falling off a bike," Earnhardt said. "You get your nerve back up to get back on it, and you're OK until you fall again."

Earnhardt also had a crash at Daytona in 1997, when Dale Jarrett clipped his bumper as they tangled with Jeff Gordon and Ernie Irvan. That sent Earnhardt into a spinning roll that left tire tracks and metal all over the backstretch. During the spin, Earnhardt was tagged hard by Ernie Irvan, the impact of which set Earnhardt's car upright where it stayed as it spun wildly into the grass infield. The crowd went silent as Earnhardt was loaded into an ambulance.

But then, it was time for the legend of the Intimidator to grow.

Earnhardt got out of the ambulance and not wearing his helmet, drove to the pits in his torn up race car.

"When I stopped, I looked at it and got in the ambulance and looked back over there and I said, 'Man, the wheels ain't knocked off that car yet,'" Earnhardt said. "I went back over there and looked at the wheels, and I told the guy in the car to fire it up. It fired up and I said, 'Get out. Unhook me, I've got to go.' We took off after 'em. You've got to get all the laps you can. That's why we're running for the championship."

That allowed him to return and finish the race in the fragments that once was the No. 3 Chevy.

"Oh, he's invincible; he's the best," said Darrell Waltrip, who trailed the crash. "He always does something spectacular, don't he? Nothing he ever does surprises me, and I mean that in the best way."

Jeff Gordon was wary when he saw Earnhardt approaching him after the race.

"At the end of the race, I see this mangled black No. 3 car coming up and I said, 'Uh-oh, what's he gonna do?'" Gordon said, only half-jokingly. "But he came up and gave me the thumbs up. I know he wanted to win the Daytona 500, but that just shows you what class he has. Don't ever count that guy out; he's the man of steel. We saw what he did with broken bones last year, and I know we're going to see that same determination for the rest of his career. It's why so many race car drivers look up to him and want to be like him."

While some drivers might not enjoy the Winston, NASCAR's version of an "All-Star Game" for the Winston Cup drivers, Earnhardt loves it.

"It's my kind of race," Earnhardt said. "Wide open, mash the gas and run for the money! This is a 'winners-only' race. Every driver out there has experienced that feeling of pulling into Victory Lane, knowing they beat the best teams in racing today. Winning the Winston means you've beaten the best of the best."

In late August of 1997, Earnhardt's fans got another scare when he mysteriously lost consciousness for a moment on the first lap of the Mountain Dew 500. He went through extensive testing to make sure he was all right.

"They did everything but check to see if I was pregnant," Earnhardt said. "Sixteen different doctors examined me, and I've received opinions from 25 doctors. I had to find out for myself personally. Not just to see if I could get back into a race car, but for my future. My future as a father, as a car owner or whatever I may do in the future of this sport. The thought did cross my mind that I might not be able to drive again. I'm pretty confident in myself that it's not going to happen again or that I've got anything wrong with me."

Earnhardt said the feelings of mortality bring a perspective.

"That crosses your mind," Earnhardt said. "You think, 'I'm going to do the MRI tomorrow. What are they going to find?' You may not be able to go on from here as a driver. But the important thing was in my time it's myself and my family. If I can't drive, being a part of it as a car owner for Dale Jr., Steve Park and the guys, that's fine. And all the friends I have in racing, you have a lot more going in life besides racing."

Alas, all the concern was put a lap down when Earnhardt erased a 20-year drought by winning the Daytona 500 in 1998.

"Yes! Yes! Yes!" said an exuberant Earnhardt in Victory Lane. "Twenty years! Can you believe it!"

He had run out of gas, suffered a cut tire, missed a lug nut—you name it, and it probably happened to Earnhardt at Daytona before 1998.

"This win is for all our fans and all the people who told me, 'Dale, this is your year,'" Earnhardt said. "There was a lot of hard work that went into this, and I have to thank every member of the Richard Childress Racing team. I have had a lot of great fans and people behind me all through the years, and I just can't thank them enough. The Daytona 500 is over. And we won it! We won it!"

Earnhardt received high-fives and handshakes from all the pit crews as he cruised down pit road toward Victory Lane.

"When you come down Pit Road after winning that race, it is so awesome," Earnhardt said. "Everyone's congratulating you, Rusty Wallace, Darrell Waltrip. . . you get that feeling. You get the teary eyes. And all—not just one team, but all the teams are out on Pit Road high-fiving you. It wore my hand out.

"This was one of the most awesome races I've ever won," Earnhardt said. "You can win races down here, but it's not like winning the Daytona 500. I've won 30 races, but the Daytona 500 overshadows all of them. It's a first. Everybody down here this week kept saying, 'This is your race. This is your year.' Watching (John) Elway win that Super Bowl pumped me up and gave me the determination and that look, and that's what it took."

His celebrity is beyond superstar status, but he'll accept the demands of being a living legend.

"The press and everybody pulling at you is a good problem to have. We manage it pretty well, and scheduling is the key to having enough time in the day to handle the business and try to enjoy the family, too," Earnhardt said.

And how does the Intimidator himself want to be remembered?

"Basically the same, as a good driver, a good father, someone who has done something right in his life," Earnhardt said. "And also, a good champion."

CHAPTER 7

BILL ELLIOTT

Elliott's excellence: Voted the NASCAR Winston Cup Series Most Popular Driver a record 12 times; won the Daytona 500 twice, in 1985 and '87; picked up the inaugural Winston Million in 1985 by winning three of the four crown jewel events (Daytona 500, Winston 500, Southern 500); won an unprecedented eleven superspeedway races in 1985; owns the fastest recorded time in a stock car, going 212.809 mph in qualifying for the 1987 Winston 500 at Talladega; finished 18th in 1998 Winston Cup points standings.

Before the clever nicknames, millions of dollars ago, Bill Elliott found out what made him tick—racing cars.

On Feb. 29, 1976, Elliott and his brothers, Ernie and Dan, took off from their Georgia home in the mountain community of Dawsonville and went to the North Carolina Speedway in Rockingham for the Carolina 500 where Bill started 34th and finished 33rd, winning $640.

Elliott actually started in the Sportsman Division in 1970. After the NASCAR debut at Rockingham in '76, Elliott's first full Winston

Cup season was 1983, although he did win the pole in his 56th qualifying attempt in the 1981 Rebel 500 at Darlington.

After 116 starts, win No. 1 came in start No. 117 at the Winston Western 500 in Riverside in 1983. Elliott tied the modern-era record with four consecutive Winston Cup wins in 1992. His single-season mark of 11 superspeedway wins 1985 was a record. In that year, he won the first-ever Winston Million, which earned him the nickname, "Million-dollar Bill."

Mainly because of injuries, Elliott had a tough time in 1998, but he still recovered for a very solid finish in the points standings. An injury in 1996 really slowed him, but in 1997 Elliott racked up 14 top-10 finishes (the most since 1993), his most top-five finishes (five since 1994) and went over the $1 million margin in winnings for the first time since 1992. On top of that, Elliott was eighth in the 1997 final points standings, this after he had fallen out of the top 10 in 1996.

"Awesome Bill from Dawsonville" (Georgia) likes having McDonald's as a sponsor, as it has made appearances easier for Elliott.

"The beer companies are usually tough from the standpoint that they want you to go to a lounge where they serve the beer," Elliott said. "That exposed me to a limited group of people. With McDonald's, however, even before they sponsored a race car, I liked the fact that I could go there and anyone could come in and visit me. With the other sponsors, I would wait outside for a while, or if I was inside and a kid came, I would have to go outside to sign something or meet them. The McDonald's deal was a whole lot better, and a whole lot easier to do than the beer companies."

Elliott also likes to dine on his sponsor's food, and he is proud that it has gotten more and more nutritious in recent years.

"I eat a good bit of McDonald's stuff everywhere I go," said Elliott, who enjoys snow skiing and flying—he has multi-engine-rated and helicopter-rated pilot licenses and owns his own planes. "I like the Filet of Fish and the regular hamburgers real well. They usually bring it out to us at the truck on race weekend. I also had a chance to attend a McDonald's convention a few weeks ago."

Elliott went into business in 1998 with Miami Dolphins quarterback Dan Marino as they operated the FIRSTPLUS No. 13 car.

"Dan has just come in to get to know racing at this point," said Elliott, who was born Oct. 8, 1955. "We're growing a good friendship there, from my standpoint. Later on, I don't know where his involvement will lead to, but it's good for the sport, having people like that, because he brings in other types of people to Winston Cup racing. Dan has limited knowledge about racing, kind of like I do about football. I watch it on Saturdays and Sundays when I can, but I don't really know much about the nitty-gritty of it. That's kind of the way it is with him. But I'm looking forward to a long relationship with him. He drove one of my cars at Talladega, and I think he has done some other things since. He did real well; he ran about 165. We went out one time and he ran about 145, and we went out again late in the afternoon, and he ran 165 or so. I think one more time and he'd have run wide open. We're trying to get him into some of the different driving schools, and maybe he can come back and try some more."

While he is part of a small team, he is trying the best he can.

"I don't have all the resources that say a Roush or a Hendrick team has, but I am trying to build and stretch out, so I can have enough resources coming in to do what I need to do," Elliott said. "Having these entities (the No. 13 and the partnership with the No. 81), gives me the opportunity to do more. The more we grow, the more we can do, and that will just help us more overall."

Elliott credits NASCAR with keeping the playing field—in this case, concrete tracks—level.

"I think everybody tries to go in and point fingers and say this guy has got an advantage, or this other guy has got an advantage, to help themselves get an advantage," Elliott said. "I think sometimes the media makes a lot of it—it's a hard question to answer. NASCAR seems to have a way of putting everything in place, to make sure nobody has an advantage."

In 1992, Elliott won at Atlanta in November as the season

ended, but finished second to Alan Kulwicki for the points championship.

"Well, I don't know which win was the most special; I look back on them, and they all had their certain points in time when they were the favorite," Elliott said. "Even going back to the Southern 500 at Darlington, the last win I had, that was exciting for me. Looking back to Atlanta that day, that was a pretty unique. If I had ended up leading a few more laps that year, it would have been different. You can't help but look back at the year and say, 'Boy, if I'd have gotten five or 10 more points here or there.' But that's the way things go."

All of the accomplishments are stepping stones to Elliott.

"They all play a part; they are all special in their own way," Elliott said. "When you go through a career, each one is a building block to the next step."

Trying to stay in shape has helped Elliott recover relatively fast from his injuries.

"Well, you gotta be in pretty good shape everywhere you go," Elliott said. "But, ironically, it's not what you'd necessarily think...for example, the shorter tracks give you less time to relax because they are harder on you corner to corner. Dover, even though it is now 400 miles, is tough. But Bristol and Martinsville are tough racetracks."

Elliott likes NASCAR's "family first" attitude, and he really likes the fact that families can travel with the drivers.

"It's gotten a lot easier since the racetracks have gotten more motor home friendly and since the racers can get those parked in a certain area; it has helped us a lot," Elliott said. "It's like a little community at the track. We don't have to get up early and fight traffic to get to the track. It has helped us maintain a good, strong family relationship and structure even though we're away from home. There are places for us to go, and a lot of the racetracks have built play areas for kids, so that has really made it nice."

How Elliott came up with his trademark No. 94 is a story in itself.

"The reason I came up with the 94 was because my nephew Casey was running it when he started his career," Elliott said. "And he passed away from cancer in January 1996. Since I wanted a nine number, and the 94 had a special meaning to our family, we went with the 94."

NASCAR's growth, driven by its constantly expanding fan base, is going to continue.

"I think NASCAR is going to expand more than we can ever imagine," Elliott said. "It's just a matter of time. Right now NASCAR is starting to explode, and you are going to see more and more tracks open up and become part of NASCAR."

Elliott really appreciates the fans.

"The fans over the years have been great; they have really taken care of me and supported me," Elliott said. "That's what this business is all about. The fans are what make this sport go, and it's been fantastic on my end."

When he won the Most Popular Driver award for the 11th time, he was equally gracious. "Well, this is the only thing I won this year," Elliott said at the time. "Winning this award for the 11th time really says something about our fans. I have said it over and over, in this sport they stick with you no matter what. When you have as many obstacles and hurdles as I did this past season, it's a great feeling to know you can count on the fans for their support. Our fans continue to be the best in the world and my many thanks go out to all of them for their dedication and support over the years."

In 1997, Elliott was named Most Popular Driver by the fans for the seventh straight year. It marked the 12th time Elliott had won the award. Richard Petty won the award nine times. Elliott has won the award every year from 1984 to 1997, with the exception of 1989 and 1990 when Darrell Waltrip won.

"After being involved in this sport for more than 20 years, our fans continue to amaze me," said Elliott, whose favorite hobby is spending time with his wife, Cindy, and their children. "They continue to support us like none other. They have supported us through the good years and the not-so-good years. Our fans are the backbone of this sport—they are the reason we do what we do. To receive this award was an unbelievable honor. Finding the proper words to express my appreciation for having won this award for a 12th time was very difficult. At that moment 'thank you' seemed hardly enough. But to our fans and fan club, my sincerest and most heartfelt thanks."

Elliott has found that the restrictor plates present a challenge at the superspeedways.

"It's hard to get used to driving Talladega and Daytona with less power than you used to have," Elliott said. "Daytona is a little less forgiving because you have to be handling well; Talladega is just a flat-out racetrack, and so even if your car isn't handling very well, you're still in a pack. And that can be really hard to deal with."

If it weren't for the restrictor plates, the speeds would have continued to climb.

"I'd say we'd probably be running 225 average or better," Elliott said. "That's a pretty fair estimate."

Regardless of the restrictor plates, Daytona is a special place for Elliott.

"The racetrack I like to figure out the best is probably Daytona," Elliott said. "You have to run it wide open, but the setup is important, and the corners can get slick. That makes it a real neat deal."

So don't think Elliott's fire no longer burns.

"I just want to go a year at a time, see how healthy I stay, and how competitive I stay. That's what it's all about," said Elliott, who lists David Pearson and Jody Ridley among his personal heroes. "You can stay in this thing for a long time, but there comes a time when you're not competitive, and you have to recognize that. It's hard to quit, I've been racing since I was about 16 or 17."

The business of racing has also grown.

"I think the business aspect has just gotten pretty expansive," Elliott said. "It really has grown. It's hard to keep up, trying to have enough avenues to keep your resources strong and to be going in the right direction. That's the hardest part, keeping your resources up to date. The guy down the street might come up with something that's a few tenths better, and it can be hard trying to deal with that."

One of Elliott's favorite competitors is the "Intimidator"—Dale Earnhardt. "Dale and I have had our scrapes, but I still enjoy racing with him; it's been a lot of fun," Elliott said. "Also, I would have to say when I had just started, I enjoyed racing against guys like David Pearson and Cale Yarborough. That was a real treat. I've been real lucky."

Racing has changed over the years in ways many could never imagine, especially in terms of technology.

"I think everything has had its evolution; the older stuff was fun to drive at the time, but the new stuff has a very different feel," Elliott said. "The new equipment, the radial tires and the aerodynamics has just become part of what you do."

Still, anyone interested in joining has to go the traditional route—hard work.

"The biggest thing is to send in a resumé, get with a team and get started," Elliott said. "There are a lot of ways to get into it. You have got to get in and work hard—sweep the floors, whatever—and go from there. Any experience you can gain, volunteering at your local track, working with something like the IROC Series on a limited deal, that's the best thing you can do."

Elliott was also the first to win the Winston Million bonus back in 1985.

"I just wanted to get it on and over with and get on down the road to the next race. When we were in Victory Lane, it was like everything happened so fast. The next day when we went home there were all these people at the shop. It was a great feeling. Everything is a stepping stone. Many people ask me what the biggest thing is in my career, and I tell 'em everything is. Winning the first race in Riverside, the championship, winning Daytona, winning Daytona again, winning the million at Darlington, even winning the Southern 500 two years ago at Darlington. All 40 wins have their place.

"What it did for me and my brothers was put us on a pedestal, so to speak. It meant even more winning it the first year it was offered up. It's hard today because of restrictor plates. Anybody can win a race at the superspeedways. We were just able to put it all together that year and we even had to overcome a problem at Talladega. I don't know if you can overcome those problems today."

Winning that million-dollar race wasn't easy.

"Earnhardt spun in front of me and I had to dodge that. Then with about a couple of laps to go, Cale Yarborough was leading and I was running second. His power steering let loose and I was able to get around him. I still had to drive hard to hold him off because he was coming fast. But I did and we won. We were all kind of in a daze in Victory Lane. It was great."

Back in 1985, at the time he won the million-dollar bonus, Elliott didn't grasp the significance of the event.

"I don't think so," Elliott said. "It was a big deal because of all the coverage, it brought a lot of media attention to this sport. It's grown a lot since then. Most of the people around the country now know a little bit about what we do. Back then we were on the cutting edge. Dale's got an excellent shot at winning this thing, probably as good of a shot since I won it in '85. He's been running well and with any kind of luck and if they get the breaks they need they can win."

After winning the first two races that year—the Daytona 500 and Winston 500—Elliott could sense that the pressure was going to rise.

"The pressure was really bad at Charlotte," Elliott said. "By the time things got to Darlington, a lot of it had died down and we were able to concentrate more on the race. We were better prepared because you go to Daytona, Talladega and Charlotte. Those happened so quick we weren't really prepared for what came at us in Charlotte. By the time we came back to Darlington we were better prepared to handle all situations. Back then I was the driver, crew chief—I wore so many hats it was unreal."

Elliott was only 19 years old going into the Winston Million year.

"I had a lot of trouble dealing with some things back then," Elliott said. "Every time somebody took me away from the race car, I resented that. I had a hard time coming to terms with that. The race car was what got me to the point where I was at. I was comfortable in the car. I was not comfortable around the media. I have never been comfortable around large groups of people, period. Even in high school, I could barely get up in front of a class and read a paragraph."

While the Ford Taurus proved to be the best car in 1998 in its debut year, Elliott had a hard time saying goodbye to the Thunderbird.

"I will really miss the T-Bird," Elliott said. "We won the championship in '88 with it, and that will always be a highlight for me. We had that great year in '85, winning 11 races and the Winston Million, but I guess the '88 championship is the season that will always stand out. We won a lot of races in '85, including the Winston Million, but the championship was the highlight."

In Bristol in April of 1997, Elliott picked up his 500th career start.

"Never did I imagine that when I first started racing I would one day have 500 starts," Elliott said. "Guess it shows I've been around for an awfully long time. But this is what I wanted to do for a living. This is a tough deal to get in, and I was fortunate to have come along when I did. No doubt about it, racing's been good to me."

The milestone almost happened in the 1996 season finale at Atlanta, but a broken leg Elliott received in an airborne crash at Talladega during the Winston 500 caused him to miss seven races.

The younger drivers push Elliott to compete as hard as he can. "These young kids come along, and they are going to continue to take it out of you, and you're going to have to work harder to stay good," Elliott said. "I'm trying to do that. You just hope you can use your experience to overcome some of the other stuff."

Talladega honored Elliott with his image on the track's first commemorative pole day ticket on Aug. 9, 1998.

"Talladega has meant a lot to me over the years," Elliott said. "We have definitely had a lot of success there, especially on qualifying day. It's quite an honor to be the driver they chose to be on their first commemorative ticket."

CHAPTER 8

JEFF GORDON

Gordon's greatness: At age 24, became second-youngest driver in history to win NASCAR Winston Cup Series championship; in 1993, won MAXX Rookie of the Year title; won seven races, eight poles and all the mid-way bonuses on way to 1995 title; led most laps and miles during the season; winner of the 1997 Daytona 500, leading a 1-2-3 Hendrick Motorsports finish with teammates Terry Labonte and Ricky Craven; won second NASCAR Winston Cup Series championship in 1997; won third NASCAR Winston Cup championship—in four years—in 1998.

Maybe Jeff Gordon is the "Rainbow Warrior" because he and his crew seem to find the pot of gold at the end of every race and almost every season. Gordon even won the final two races of the 1998 season after he had already clinched the points title during the midway point of the second-to-the-last race of the season.

Felix Sabates, owner of the No. 40, No. 42 and No. 46 Chevys, says Gordon is simply a great driver.

"I think Jeff Gordon is the best driver of all time," Sabates said.

"I think they've got the best crew of all time. If they had been driving a Ford this year (in 1998), they might be undefeated. I think he's the best driver who's ever driven a stock car. I'm in a Chevrolet, and I know we're at a disadvantage, but we can't complain about it because Gordon's in a Chevrolet, and he's kicking everybody's butt."

Gordon has plenty of fans. Yet he gets booed more than any driver. Why? He's young, handsome, married to a beautiful woman, and he's rich. But he's also a smart, well-spoken Christian man who is as active as anyone in charitable causes. He's also won the points championship three of the past four years.

Gordon was the first driver to top the $6 million mark for one season, which he did in winning the points championship in 1997, claiming the Winston Million with an August win at the Darlington Raceway.

He won the points championship in 1995 and came just 37 points short of defending his title, as Terry Labonte won it all in 1996. In 1997, Gordon, from Pittsboro, Indiana, faced a stiff challenge from Dale Jarrett, who finished second, 14 points behind Gordon.

Gordon is the youngest NASCAR Winston Cup Series champion in the modern era, having achieved that distinction at age 24. He was the youngest titleholder since Bill Rexford won the title at age 23 in 1950.

Gordon began racing go-karts and quarter-midgets at age 5. In 1979 and 1981 he was the quarter-midget national champion. In 1990 he won the USAC midget championship. In 1992 on the NASCAR Busch Series Grand National Division circuit he won a record 11 poles. He also made his NASCAR Winston Cup Series debut at Atlanta, qualifying 21st and finishing 31st. In 1993 he was the series' Rookie of the Year.

"My parents, actually my stepfather and my mother, were the ones that got me into racing," Gordon said. "Now, the sport has grown into a business, and they still support me. They don't come to as many races, but my stepfather works for a company that's involved."

The 5-foot-6, 150-pound Gordon, who was born on Aug. 4, 1971, won his first race at Charlotte in the Coca-Cola 600 in 1994. He followed that up by winning the inaugural Brickyard 400.

Gordon's hobbies are water-skiing, snow-skiing, and playing racquetball and video games.

Among the adversity Gordon has had to deal with were allegations in 1998 that Gordon's team was illegally treating tires—tests on those tires revealed nothing.

Larry McReynolds, the crew chief for Mike Skinner (and former Dale Earnhardt crew chief), knows Gordon is cutting no corners.

"Jeff Gordon is racing his guts out every weekend," McReynolds said. "Ray Evernham really knows how to handle Jeff. They have a great engine program, a great chassis program and a great aero program. And if he goes into the pits in fifth, he knows he's got a pretty good shot at leaving in the lead. That's the thing about today's competition, it's so close, I'm talking decimals."

NASCAR Winston Cup series crew chief Andy Graves (for Terry Labonte's car) knows Gordon as well as anyone.

"He's a pretty good guy," Graves said. "From living with him for five years, everyone has their downfalls, but Jeff is a really neat individual. It's a shame he's become so popular and people want to take shots at him because he's really a great guy. I've seen Jeff in the zone before, and when he really wants to do something, that's the way he gets."

Philippe Lopez said Gordon's team is simply strong from top to bottom.

"They've got a lot of talent all the way through that team," Lopez said. "I couldn't even point out a weak link, that's how strong they are. I know that's why teams get jealous. We all have to catch up, and it won't be overnight. Look back, there's always a super team. Beating that team is going to take more work, with everyone working overtime, just trying to get better."

Jerry Nadeau, a Winston Cup rookie in the 1998 season, said Gordon's detractors are looking for something to pick at—and even questioning whether the 24 car is playing by the same rules—when in fact they should just be offering respect for the Rainbow Warrior's effort.

"Instead of looking at someone winning and wondering why he's winning, people should just appreciate it," Nadeau said. "Gordon wins those races because he and his team are good. I wish I were in his shoes. That's a big accomplishment."

Fellow driver Mark Martin—Gordon's chief rival for the 1998 season—said Gordon's talent is special.

"I'm a Jeff Gordon fan," Martin said. "He's a fine fellow, and it hurts me to hear him booed because he is good. I guess I've been fortunate enough to have success, but not so much that a large number of people would dislike me. That guy's awesome."

Gordon takes the boos in stride, continuing to find a way to focus on the positive.

"There's definitely positive and negative things that come along with success," Gordon said. "But for the most part, it's been a very positive experience. I know there are a million people who would trade places with me. But there are things that are tough about it; you definitely lose a lot of your privacy. There are always a lot of rumors and such that are being spread around to bring you from the top and break your team down. It's hard when you know the truth. That's been the hardest thing, and as long as we keep winning races, then I'll keep a smile on my face."

The large load of success might well be the primary reason Gordon is booed.

"If that's what comes along with it, then it's almost like an incentive for me to get more boos," Gordon said. "That means we're doing something good for our team. I've heard some pretty foul language. People call me names and stuff, but again, I don't take it personally. I laugh about it and say, 'Hey, these race fans are loyal, and that's the way it is.' I've learned to accept it and try to understand it. If I knew I had done something wrong, something bad, and I got booed, then it would bother me a lot more. But by just going out there and racing and winning races, it really doesn't affect me. I think everybody likes a winner, but nobody likes somebody to win more than they think they should. I've got a lot of fans out there who are cheering. But everybody pulls for their driver, their car, their team. They want their guy to win. And, in a way, they want me to lose because I've been the one winning the races here lately."

Darrell Waltrip—a Gordon fan—knows about being booed, but is now one of the fans' favorite racers.

"When I was in (that) position in the '80s," Waltrip says, "the problem I had was that I was a smart aleck. I wanted to be cute all the time. I was always saying something to tick somebody off. That was my nature. But I enjoyed it. I liked being in trouble. It set me away from the rest of the crowd. So I deserved what I got. But here's a kid who doesn't deserve to be booed. He deserves to be cheered and appreciated, and I for one cheer him and appreciate him. Everybody's scared of Jeff Gordon. The competition is scared of him. Dale Earnhardt is scared to death of him because he's going to win more championships and more races than he did, and more money...Do you know anything bad about Jeff Gordon? I don't know of anything. He's too good for his own good. When I was booed so much, I was beating all the old favorites, and I think it's the same thing now. In the '80s, up until '87 and '88 maybe, most people who know about the sport know I was a fairly unpopular driver and a fairly controversial driver. I was always in the middle of things, good and bad. I got booed profoundly, just at the mention of my name. Just like Gordon, people walked around with 'Anybody but Waltrip' shirts on. That will happen when you're a dominant driver. That just goes with being successful. I don't know why that's the way it is in our sport, not really in other sports. The fans really have a love-hate relationship with the drivers in our sport, more than any other athletes out there today."

The Intimidator has been booed as well.

"I remember riding around in a convertible with Earnhardt in '93 or '94 during driver introductions and hearing the boos for him," Gordon said. "He had just come off a championship and won five or six races the year before. It was like they didn't want him to win another championship. During that ride he looked at me, smiled, and said, 'Hey, as long as they're making noise.' And it's true. I'd much rather people make loud noise, no matter what it is, than to introduce me and nobody clapped, cheered or booed."

Gordon said he would have liked the chance to race in the "old" days of NASCAR.

"Obviously, I would have loved to race against Richard Petty," Gordon said. "I was in my first Winston Cup race in his last Winston Cup race. I would have loved to race him in his prime; that would have been very exciting. I don't know if I could have kept up with him. There were also David Pearson, Ned Jarrett, Benny Parsons; the list goes on and on . . . they were guys who were winning a lot of races, and I would have loved to race against them."

NASCAR's continued growth is amazing to Gordon, who sees nothing but bright skies for the sport in the future.

"I think NASCAR is doing an excellent job marketing-wise and really doing a lot to help the sport grow, even in the scheduling," Gordon said. "I feel like I play a role, just like every other driver does. But, yes, I'm young, and I've got some great sponsors who are using me in advertising. And being in *People* magazine helps me and also helps the whole sport. And there are a lot of things that are going on to help this sport get to where we want it to be—up there with the NBA, NFL. I think it can happen."

The current crop of veterans have lent their expertise and experience to Gordon.

"When I need advice about racing, I really rely on the people that are closest to us," Gordon said. "When I first came into the sport I would go to my teammates, Kenny Schrader and then Ricky Rudd. And because we had such good equipment, we got to race with guys like Dale Earnhardt, Mark Martin, Bill Elliott, and I learned a lot. Off the track, the business side of things, Dale Earnhardt has taught me a lot about scheduling other things involved with the business side of the sport."

While Gordon seems to be in the front at the end of most races, he claims it is important to handle not being out front during the early stages of the race—to be patient and not blow a chance by getting careless.

"Every race has something different to offer," Gordon said. "If you watch races closely, we're not always in the front. We have to battle to get there. And Victory Lane never gets boring; it's always exciting, the pure joy and thrill of success and to feel what it's like to claim victory."

Gordon knows kids should look to their parents first, but admits he takes pride in being a good role model.

"I think that some athletes have said that the parents should be the role models, not the athletes," Gordon said. "I think that it's very important for the parents to do that, but any person that's in the limelight is going to have people look up to him/her, kids especially. I try and live my life at the racetrack the same as I do away from the track. I know God has helped me deal with a lot of pressures in life in general, and especially driving that race car. I couldn't do it without Him. I know getting to heaven is the most important thing. That's how I prioritize things; God is No. 1, and family is No. 2."

The time demands are something Gordon might never get used to.

"I definitely feel like there's not enough time in the day and not enough days in the week and the year, that's for sure," Gordon said. "You know, every year we try and get more organized and do a better job with scheduling. It's one of the most important things we do in the off-season, schedule a year and a year-and-a-half in advance, even schedule when I'm going to take a vacation, or when I'm going to work out, and when I'm going to the shop. We try and schedule every week. It makes your off-time more efficient, I guess."

Gordon enjoys sharing his Christian faith whenever he has the opportunity. "I do love to speak in churches, giving my testimony," he said.

Gordon appreciates his crew—the Rainbow Warriors.

"I try to go by and see them and take my team out to lunch every chance I get," Gordon said. "When we win a championship, or like when we won the Winston Million and things like that, I have done things like get rings. We got Winston Million rings for all the guys on the team, rings for the Winston Cup championship. And I had some special leather jackets made after the championship last year. It's great, we get with the sponsors and really try to give back to the team. And not to mention, the better we do on the track, the better their bonus is. And I try and kick in at the halfway point in the season and at the end of the season."

There are changes on the horizon for NASCAR. Some wonder if that will include indoor racing.

"You see football stadiums with domes on them, and that could be the next step," Gordon said. "It would be nice as far as weather is concerned, but one thing you have to do with race cars—because I have raced indoors with sprint cars and midgets—is you have to do something about the fumes. At Bristol that's already a concern for the drivers, and of course it's a concern for the fans, too. That would be the biggest concern of mine."

One of Gordon's biggest rivals—and someone for whom Gordon has a lot of respect—is Dale Earnhardt.

"Dale and I get along great," Gordon said. "We play with each other back and forth at the racetrack. Since I won a championship, I think we have a little more in common. With schedules, I don't see him off the track. But once we're on the track, we're both pretty competitive."

The key to success, Gordon said, is no single thing. Indeed, a good team must have good team members, good equipment and a good driver.

"It's not one thing that makes us succeed; it's all those things," Gordon said. "With the competition in Winston Cup racing, it's all got to be together to make a winner and a champion."

At this point in his career, Gordon has wins on all kinds of courses.

"I grew up racing on short tracks, so I have more experience," Gordon said. "I enjoy superspeedways—the drafting is really fun. The road courses are something new, and I'm learning to enjoy them. But the key is that my team gives me great race cars every week."

While actual time behind the wheel is important, other factors contribute to a driver's success.

"Seat time is definitely important," Gordon said. "But patience is also very important. It's easy to get down. This is a select sport, and only a few drivers make it to this level, and it does take time to start winning. I think patience was the biggest thing I was lacking as a rookie and able to learn over the years."

In 1998, Gordon was on a tear. While Mark Martin was having the year of his life, Gordon was having a year for the ages. He became the seventh driver in the Winston Cup's modern era with four straight wins. Gordon came from the back to win, won on a road course and even in Michigan where he overtook an emotional Martin, who was racing the same week his father, stepmother and half-sister died in a plane wreck.

The following week, Gordon finally fell from the top spot—but still landed in fifth at Bristol.

"I've been saying this is a Russian roulette track," Gordon said. "At any moment, the bomb can go off or the trigger can have the bullet and be an explosion. This place is just being at the right place at the right time and being lucky. It's important to have a car that is running up front. Last year we had that, and that didn't get us out of trouble. You have to be smart; you have to be patient. What happens here is tempers flare so easy. Tempers can flare instantly, so what you have to do is always control that. Guys who can do that will come out of here with a good finish."

Gordon was the first driver since Martin in 1993 to win four straight races. Others who have done it are Cale Yarborough in 1976, Darrell Waltrip in 1981, Dale Earnhardt in 1987, Harry Gant in 1991 and Bill Elliott in 1992. Richard Petty won 10 straight races in 1967, but that was before NASCAR entered its modern era in 1972 with a schedule ranging between 29-33 races a season. Prior to that, NASCAR ran about 60 races a season, many of just 100 miles on weeknights.

The records aren't that important to Gordon, but the competition—and the challenge—are.

"It certainly keeps me fired up," Gordon said. "I love doing things that haven't been done before. It's really neat for the team to be part of something like that. You feel like you are making history in this sport. When you are on a roll and on a streak, you are the guy to beat and the guy everybody looks at and is measuring themselves against."

During his streak, Gordon won with a dominating performance at Pocono, capitalized on bad luck by Dale Jarrett in the Brickyard 400 and continued his road course excellence at Watkins Glen. In the Pepsi 400 at Michigan Speedway, Gordon believed he got lucky when his crew made some important changes on the final pit stop, helping him take the lead from Mark Martin in the closing laps of the race.

NASCAR legend Harry Gant went so far as to call Gordon the greatest driver in NASCAR history at this stage of his career.

"To hear that means a lot," Gordon said. "I've learned quite a bit from Harry. It's hard for me to really comprehend what Harry is saying. I don't really try to compare myself with other drivers as to who is the best. I just try to make sure our efforts are the best so we can win races and championships."

Winning the 1997 Daytona 500 brought some excitement out of Gordon. Consider his comments at the time:

"Am I here? Is this happening? This is awesome!" Gordon said. "When I won the Brickyard 400 in 1994 I thought that no moment could ever pass that one. This one has. I know this is only my fifth season in Winston Cup, but I appreciate each year more and more. I'm so happy."

From Victory Lane, Gordon talked by cell phone to team owner Rick Hendrick. While Hendrick cars went 1-2-3 (Gordon was followed by teammates Terry Labonte and Ricky Craven), it was a hard time for Hendrick, whose leukemia had yet to go into remission.

"I just wanted to glorify God and make this a great day for Rick

Hendrick," Gordon said. "I never could have imagined that this day would be what it has turned out to be. To win the Daytona 500, to go on that list of names is a real honor, but to run one, two, three (with Labonte and Craven) was probably more of an honor to do that for Rick Hendrick. I came driving up (to Victory Lane), and all I could think was, 'Man, I wish I could talk to Rick.' All of a sudden I see someone on the phone, and I say he's got to be talking to Rick. So I grabbed the phone out of his hand, and I'm screaming, 'We won the Daytona 500.' And I shut the engine off, and he was like, 'Who is this?' And I said, 'This is Jeff.' And he started going nuts. That made my day. I'll tell you, to hear the laughter and the joy in his voice, that's what it was all about."

Ray Evernham said the mutual respect he and Gordon have for each other is a big part of their cooperative success.

"I think it is, honestly, respect," Evernham said. "I think he's the greatest, and I think he thinks I'm the greatest. And we have that mutual respect."

Gordon simply loves what he does and plans to continue doing it the best he can.

"I saw Magic Johnson interviewed one time, and I'll never forget this," Gordon said. "He said what drove him and what kept him playing basketball for so many years was the pure love and desire to win."

The points championship in 1997 was Gordon's second in three years.

"You just have to be consistent and win races, and that's tough to do because a lot of times when you win a lot of races you're also taking chances on the other races and usually that will cost you a lot of points and positions," Gordon said.

The weeks leading up to the final race where Gordon clinched the title, were rough.

"My nerves were shot," Gordon said. "Every muscle in my body was tense. I really and honestly hadn't slept for two weeks, ever since Phoenix. I had basically been saying, 'Yeah, yeah, I'm fine.' I have to do that because you can't let your competitors, you can't let the media, you can't let anybody know that things could be getting to you, or they will know where your weaknesses are. I still felt good about what our chances were to win the championship. But I was like, 'Oh boy, what have we done? What have I done? I go out and wreck a great race car on pit road.' Then we go out with the back-up race car and had a shot at a top-10 qualifying and made a mistake and dropped some oil on the track and ended up barely getting into the show…that's what makes it so much sweeter, so satisfying to go through a day like that and then back it up. I'm sure a lot of people had doubts, and a lot of people were counting us out and saying, 'Hey, we got them right where we want them.'"

The 24 car stays out front because no one on the team is ever caught sleeping.

"Quite honestly, the biggest thing you need to be on guard for is success itself," Evernham said. "Because success has a tendency to lull people to sleep. Everyone has to realize that you're not going to have an advantage just because of your presence; you're still going to have to work for it. I think that's the thing that concerns me the most. You cannot assume that you're going to be good just because of your reputation."

While Gordon has received plenty of attention, other drivers are getting plenty of coverage as well.

"I've been watching the news," Gordon said. "I'm not the only guy they've put on there. I've seen (Dale) Earnhardt. He's still the man. They still utilize him and his talents. I saw something that said he's like a rock star, and it's the truth. He's Earnhardt, and people come to see him. It's the same thing with Mark Martin and Dale Jarrett. I'm glad to be at the top of the list, but I don't feel like I'm the No. 1 guy on the list. I feel like in the mix of maybe a top-five or top-10 list."

Following the 1997 season, Gordon cleaned up at the NASCAR banquet, where he was honored for winning the points championship.

"Money is not a priority for me and never has been," Gordon said at the NASCAR awards banquet where he picked up enough bonus money to push his earnings for 1997 past the $6 million mark. "That's not what keeps you happy. I like to win, I like to compete and I like to drive a race car. That's what makes me happy in my career.

"Our guys have a lot of confidence," Gordon said. "This race team got off on the right foot where we had success early. That helped keep good people, and it also helped attract other good people. It's youth, it's confidence, it's great leadership by Ray (and Rick Hendrick). I think all those things have helped us overcome the disadvantages that other teams have seen. I think we've really been able to do a great job in the pits and really communicate well. We've got good race cars, but it goes back to the people who are building them and Ray and me communicating and trying to get the most out of the cars."

Gordon was also voted a "Future Legend" of NASCAR.

"This is an awful big load to carry on my shoulders for the next 50 years, so bear with me," Gordon said. "I just hope I can fulfill the honor because those are big shoes to fill. I'm excited because the fans and the media are always asking me questions like 'What about all the boos?. . .You're disliked so much. . .' It's just great that the fans have chosen me to win this award. I hope I can do a good job of taking this sport into the next 50 years. I look forward to being around for a long time and hopefully being a major player. It's very, very exciting."

Gordon's passion for NASCAR itself is matched only by his passion for winning.

"I certainly didn't grow up knowing a lot about NASCAR stock car racing, but for the short period of time that I have gotten to know about it, I know it's where my heart's at," Gordon said. "It's where I want to be for a long time, and I've had a lot of different offers to do a lot of different things. I love where I'm at; I've got a great situation with a wonderful car owner in Rick Hendrick and a great team led by Ray Evernham and wonderful sponsors. I've always believed you stick with what works. I feel like things are going well, and I'm going to stick with this for a long time."

The high pressure to win from the public and the media won't faze Gordon.

"I always put more pressure on myself than anyone else ever could anyway," Gordon said. "I want to win as much or more than anyone else on this team. There's no way anybody could put anything on my shoulders that either hasn't been there in the past or could weigh me down any more than already. I think it's how well you handle the pressures in those types of situations that sets you apart from some of the other guys. I'm obviously the type of person who can put those things out of my mind and just focus on driving the race car and winning races."

CHAPTER 9

RON HORNADAY

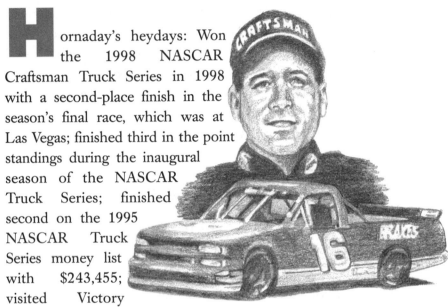

Hornaday's heydays: Won the 1998 NASCAR Craftsman Truck Series in 1998 with a second-place finish in the season's final race, which was at Las Vegas; finished third in the point standings during the inaugural season of the NASCAR Truck Series; finished second on the 1995 NASCAR Truck Series money list with $243,455; visited Victory Lane six times in the inaugural season of the NASCAR Truck Series; won 1996 series championship; won a season-best seven races in 1997 season.

Saugus Speedway is a familiar stop to only those who know the area of southern California sandwiched between Los Angeles and the High Desert area of the Antelope Valley.

But to those who know Ron Hornaday, it is the birthplace of his racing career, one that has led him to the top of the heap in NASCAR's Craftsman Truck Series.

"I started racing a little dirt car," Hornaday said. "I actually started by helping other people; I worked on their cars. Then, I started at a little old dirt track at the fairgrounds. My father raced, and I got into it early with motorcycles. I raced motocross for about eight years. But I went to Pro Class and got hurt my second time out."

Hornaday traced the shoes of his father, Ron Sr., who also won the NASCAR Winston West Championship, to the NASCAR Modified stock car title at Saugus. Hornaday was twice the NASCAR Featherlite Southwest Tour Champion.

"I've raced the local Saturday night stuff. I ran the Southwest tour, the Winston West and a couple of Cup races," said Hornaday, who was born on June 20, 1958. "Then there's the Truck Series. I would race anything with two wheels. I enjoy all competitive sports. I raced '88 to '95 in the Southwest tour—two championships and two seconds."

Joining the truck series in 1995 driving for Teresa Earnhardt, Hornaday was third in the points title, behind friends Mike Skinner and Joe Ruttman.

Driving for the "Intimidator"—Dale Earnhardt—hasn't been intimidating to Hornaday.

"I have a lot of direct contact with him," Hornaday said. "The only races he goes to are the ones that we are racing at together. He's got a lot of things going on in a busy schedule, and his time is his time. He's got a lot of faith in our team and doesn't need to be there."

In 1996 Hornaday dominated, winning four times and finishing on the lead lap in all but one of the 24 contests. He also became the first-ever truck series driver to win on a short track, a superspeedway and a road course in a single season. He also became the first truck series driver to win a second series championship by moving up from fourth to second place on the final two laps during the season finale in Las Vegas, holding off eventual race winner Jack Sprague by three points, even though Sprague, who won the 1997 points title, won that final race in '98.

"I'd rather run road courses; it's more of a challenge, but you get the same effect of winning as you do on an oval," Hornaday said. "I've won more on road courses, I know that."

In 1997, Hornaday led the Craftsman Truck tour with seven wins, but struggles early in the season bounced him back to fifth place in the points standings.

Hornaday is known for being very strong when it comes to restarts, something he claims is mechanical, mental and also gets better with experience.

"Through short-track racing, I've started in the back before," Hornaday said. "Coming from my motorcycle days and Saugus Speedway, I learned to pass from the back. There's a lot of yellow flags on short track racing, so you learn fast or you get left behind."

The truck series continues to grow and has a fan base that rivals both the Busch Grand National and Winston Cup tours.

"I'm very pleased with the enthusiasm of the truck series," Hornaday said. "I'd like to see a lot more people in it. I enjoy signing all those autographs. I learned a long time ago that the fan makes the sport. And the more you can give them the quality time, it's just going to make NASCAR that much bigger."

The competitors on the truck series are, for the most part, a pretty close-knit group.

"I have a blast," Hornaday said. "When you go to the racetrack and see all your friends and the competitors on the track, you definitely have a lot of fun."

Likewise, if other drivers ask Hornaday questions, any answer he gives will be honest.

"If any other truck driver comes over to me, I'll let them know what I have in my truck," Hornaday said. "I want the races to be competitive. That comes from owning my own chassis company. You can't lie about what's in your car because if you do, they'll never buy another car from you."

Don't be fooled into thinking Hornaday is surprised by the truck series' success and popularity.

"Not at all, anytime you put NASCAR and a series with a sponsor like Craftsman behind it, it's going to be big," Hornaday said. "I'm happy for it, particularly for the fans."

The truck series has its own version of Daytona.

"Bristol, in the truck series, is called our Daytona with its high banks," Hornaday said. "Bristol is not a hard track, but it takes a lot out of a driver. It's a demanding track."

Hornaday's affection for Bristol began long before he started racing there.

"When I was short track racing on the West Coast, I would watch races on television from Bristol and think, 'Wow, what a place; I can't wait to get a chance to race there.' I still feel that way every time I pull into the place. What Burton Smith and his staff have done at Bristol is amazing. It is one of the finest tracks in the country. When you win at Bristol, it is big. Bristol is real fast. You have to stay focused and keep calm. Things happen real quick. You and the truck take a pounding for two hours."

There's also a lot of rough driving at times in the truck series. Since the races don't travel as many miles as the Winston Cup cars do, it brings more of a sense of urgency for the truck drivers.

"It just depends how you look at it," Hornaday said. "Depending on the length of the race, to get to the front you have less time. The Winston Cup races are all 400 to 500 miles long. But that's what makes it exciting..."

Hornaday has driven all kinds of cars. The only problem is when he has to pull "double-duty" between the Busch and truck series.

"It is only when you do them the same day," Hornaday said. "If you're in a truck that day, you run a truck. If you're in a Busch car, you're in a Busch car. It's tough to do them both, or at least give 100 percent at both the same day."

Still, there are differences.

"Just the aerodynamics—the cars have better aerodynamic packages than the trucks do," Hornaday said. "They're actually a harder vehicle to drive because of the wheelbase, compression, everything."

Although his goals lay apart from the truck series, he still wants to make an even bigger mark on the truck series than he already has.

"My goals are to someday be a Winston Cup champion,"

Hornaday said. "But for now I'd like to see myself as a seven-time NASCAR Craftsman Truck Series champion."

Hornaday took several rides on the Busch Grand National Tour for Robert Pressley in 1998 while Pressley was pursuing Winston Cup Series points.

"Anything you do just gives you more experience," Hornaday said. "When they called me because Robert has other commitments for Winston Cup, we had an off weekend for the truck series, so you've got to do it. We go back to some of those places with the trucks, and that just gives much more experience for the truck for the championship. So it's a pleasure."

The Busch Grand National car is also different from the trucks.

"You've got a shorter wheelbase than the truck," Hornaday said. "You've got the downforce of the Winston Cup car and maybe a little bit more because you get to run the air dams lower and you have a bigger spoiler. It's going to be different. Basically the motors are the same as the truck. It's a smaller carburetor, so you won't be as fast down the straightaway. You're going to have to make up with a lot of corner speed."

The Hornadays moved across the country to Mooresville, North Carolina, the state that has proven to be the hub in this country for racing.

"I live on Lake Norman, and I love to water-ski and watch my wife catch every fish in the lake," Hornaday said. "That's when we get a weekend off. And I love to watch other NASCAR events on TV."

While the racing success and commitments keep him busy, Hornaday has made sure to keep his career a family affair.

"Racing actually helps my family out," said Hornaday, who enjoys spending time with his wife, Lindy, and the couple's two children. "I've been racing all my life, and my family comes all over the country with me. And NASCAR is nice enough to let members of my family come all over with me. So, it actually helps my family. I take them to all the races and all of the appearances that they want to go to."

Drivers are proud to represent their vehicle manufacturers, whether it be Ford, Dodge and Chevy in the truck series or Ford, Pontiac and Chevy in the Winston Cup and Busch Grand National series.

"Definitely, they have their own points program," Hornaday said. "I've always driven Chevrolets, and when you beat those other manufacturers out there, it's a real feather in the manufacturer's cap."

Those feathers don't come from luck—only hard work.

"We don't believe in lucky charms anymore; wherever the Lord takes us is fine," Hornaday said. "I used to be superstitious, but not anymore."

Some young drivers are willing to forego their schooling to drive. Hornaday encourages kids to finish whatever schooling goals they have before they take to the racing circuit full time.

"There's all kinds of good schools you can go to and learn about racing," Hornaday said. "But the best is to finish school first."

Hornaday's television commercial work has drawn rave reviews from fans. However, Hornaday claims he was the one who was fortunate just to be involved with such projects.

"I had more fun making that commercial than you would imagine," he said.

Though his schedule is demanding, the constant stream of hard work keeps Hornaday in shape.

"I just stay active by helping to work on the trucks, and I have a house on the water and water-ski a lot," Hornaday said.

When Hornaday beat out Skinner in Skinner's 1996 bid to defend his points title, Hornaday got only respect.

"You out-finished us, you out-drove us," Skinner said to Hornaday. "You deserved this deal. If we couldn't win it, I'd want it to be you."

In May of 1997, Hornaday had already reached the million-dollar earning mark on the truck series.

"It's exciting to think we can win a million dollars in such a short time," Hornaday said at the time. "It says a lot about this series, and what NASCAR has done with it. Thanks to Dale and Teresa Earnhardt and a great NAPA Brakes team, this is possible for us."

In 1997, when heated rival Jack Sprague won the points title as Hornaday came just short in defending his title, Hornaday showed a lot of class.

"My hat's off to Sprague and the whole Hendrick team," Hornaday said. "They have earned the championship. I think if you compare his season this year to our season last year, you will see that the stats are very similar. I have enjoyed racing with Sprague this year and look forward to battling him for the championship next year."

The rivalry with Sprague has kind of toned down—at least off the track.

"It's kind of a joking deal, now," Hornaday said. "If you watch the last couple of races, my truck's been coming out with no scratches, and his truck's been having the tire marks on it, so I can rib him a little bit. When you get two teams with the quality or caliber that we have like Hendrick's team and Dale Earnhardt, Inc., you're going to have some (rivalry). We've been qualifying side by side every week, we've been racing for the win every week, and we've been racing for top-fives.

"We had a long talk just before Bristol, Jack Sprague and I did, and Mike Wallace sat in on it," Hornaday said. "We kind of let Jack know that when we go out there, we're not doing it to make enemies, we're going out there to race hard and that's my driving style. You can't help that and vice versa; you've got your driving style. We've got to keep it on the racetrack, whatever it is. We're a big family after that race, and whatever happens on that track, you can't take it out on my family, and I can't take it out on yours. Once it's said and done you can still be mad, but we've got to go on to the next week.

"Jack's already changed for the better," Hornaday said. "He's a champion, and he knows it. When it comes down to the last lap, I don't think Jack will have respect for me, and I won't have much respect for him. But off the racetrack we understand each other. On the racetrack, there's still a lot of points involved and still a lot of money involved. You've got a lot of corporate sponsors who want to see their truck win. Whatever happens that last lap happens."

The two aren't the kind of "buddies" who would hang out together, but reaching an understanding on attitudes did a lot for goodwill among the truck drivers.

"I've got a different lifestyle," said Hornaday. "I ride my Harley, and he rides his—we just ride on different sides of the street. We don't see eye to eye on some things, but we see eye to eye on racing. We both like to race hard and to win."

CHAPTER 10

KENNY IRWIN

Irwin info: Won 1994 USAC Silver Crown Series Rookie of Year Award; won NASCAR Craftsman Truck Series Cintas Rookie of the Year Award in 1997; won Raybestos Winston Cup Rookie of the Year in 1998; won first Winston Cup pole in the final race of the 1998 season in Atlanta at NAPA 500; finished No. 28 in points—the same number as on the side of his car—for the 1998 Winston Cup points standings; drove to Bud Pole in his second NASCAR Craftsman Truck Series start at Richmond International Raceway; posted two NASCAR Craftsman Truck Series victories (Texas and Metro Dade-Homestead) in 1997; in 1996, he qualified on outside pole in first NASCAR Winston Cup Series race (Richmond International Raceway).

A winner at every level, Kenny Irwin hasn't slowed down as he completed his initial Winston Cup season in 1998 with Rookie of the Year honors.

In September of 1997, Irwin qualified for the outside pole in his first-ever Winston Cup race, at Richmond International. Irwin led that race for 12 laps and finished eighth, becoming the only modern-era driver to start on the front row and finish among the top 10 in his first Winston Cup race.

"I've been very lucky to have both my first truck race and my first Winston Cup race at Richmond," said Irwin, who was born Aug. 5, 1969. "I had run laps there before, running open-wheel races and Silver Crown events there."

If you want to call Kenny Irwin Jr.'s ride meteoric, you'd better be talking about a pretty darn fast meteor because Irwin's success has come fast at each and every level.

In 1997 during his first full season on the NASCAR Craftsman Truck Series Tour, Irwin won the Cintas Rookie of the Year Award. In only his second truck race, he won the pole.

Only three races into the 1997 season, Irwin was in Victory Lane after claiming the Florida Dodge Dealers 400K at the Metro-Dade Homestead Complex in Florida.

"You know, I really didn't think it could come this early; I mean, it's only the third race of the season," Irwin said at the time. "But it did, and I'll take it."

The season was tough at times, with a wreck in May and several finishes out of the top 10.

"It's tough. Not just being a rookie, but being in a truck, too," Irwin said. "Then you throw 36 other guys out there with me, and it's a really tough deal."

In 1998, taking over the No. 28 Ford Taurus, he won the Winston Cup Rookie of the Year honors.

Team owner Robert Yates made the decision to bring Irwin to the Winston Cup series.

"The real decision here is about opportunity," Yates said in a press conference at Indianapolis Motor Speedway announcing the signing of Irwin in August of 1997. "It's about, 'Come on, we can do it.' So today, Kenny Irwin, come on, we can do it. It hasn't been the easiest decision. I make a lot of decisions on my two feet, but I always take the team into mind. I love challenges. And I want to bring a guy who has been to the top at every level he's been to the top of this mountain. This is our pick, and this is what we're going to make work."

Joining an established team made Irwin feel comfortable immediately.

"I think there would be a lot more pressure if I was joining a brand-new start-up team," said Irwin, whose hometown is Indianapolis. "At least I know the 28 car can win races."

Irwin has almost always been a race car driver.

"When I was about 6 years old, we moved into quarter-midget racing in Indiana," Irwin said. "We ran that for about three years, then moved up to go-karts and on down the line—very similar to Terry Labonte, Jeff Gordon, other drivers whose family got them involved at a very young age, and then they had the desire to keep going on in the sport."

Irwin totaled eight wins and 20 career second places (plus 59 top-five finishes and 87 top-10 finishes) during five full seasons on the USAC Skoal National Midget Series, winning the championship in 1996.

"When I was 16 we started in road racing, IMSA division," Irwin said. "We ran that for a few years. About the same time, we bought a midget and started doing that. I ran that for a year and got a ride. I ran all three divisions in USAC. That's how I got the opportunity in the truck series, with the Thunder Series and trying to get noticed on the USAC circuit."

He also has four career wins on the USAC Silver Crown series and seven USAC Stoops/Freightliner Spring Car series victories and earned that circuit's Rookie of the Year Award in 1993. In 1994, Irwin was tabbed the USAC Silver Crown Rookie of the Year.

"In USAC, they had a lot of TV exposure; we ran a lot of races in a lot of different divisions," Irwin said. "Making those transitions made it easier for me to go to the truck series. It was just something different to drive. I recommend running USAC whether you want to go Indy or NASCAR. Wherever you want to go, USAC is a great training ground."

Leaving the open-wheel division for NASCAR wasn't a difficult choice.

"I had the opportunity to go to the IRL, but a few years ago I decided to try to get into NASCAR. I just feel like right now, NASCAR is where the opportunities are for me."

Going from behind the wheel of a truck to a Winston Cup series took some adjustment.

"The weight of the cars is different," Irwin said. "If you are familiar with a Silver Crown USAC car, they drive more like that than any other car I've driven. I've driven some ASA Late Models, but even they are not much the same. They are a lot like the Silver Crown dirt cars."

However, going from open-wheel to trucks wasn't as difficult.

"The trucks aren't any more physically demanding than open-wheel," Irwin said. "In open-wheel we run 70 or 80 times a year. Of course, the races are a lot shorter. During the race, trucks are more demanding because we run 300 or 400 laps, but the off track is more demanding in the NASCAR program, all the things that go with driving at this level. It was a little overwhelming when I first got into it, but it just takes a little time to get used to."

Irwin was also able to race against arguably the top truck driver ever, Ron Hornaday.

"Without a doubt Ron Hornaday is the strongest team driver," Irwin said. "I think that the competition is getting tougher every year, especially when you see the number of trucks at the first few races."

With the move up to the Winston Cup in 1998, Irwin was also able to race in his own backyard at the Brickyard 400.

"When you're watching from the grandstands, it looks a lot easier than when you get in the car," Irwin said. "I've watched several races here, and I've been all around the racetrack, but I've never driven around it until we came here to race in the Brickyard. And now, I know it's definitely a lot tougher than what I anticipated. A lot of people ask me if there's a lot more pressure here, coming back to Indianapolis. But for me, it's a lot more relaxing because I get to see my mom and dad a lot more and get to stay at their house."

Getting to know the different drivers as he has moved up each level is akin to becoming acclimated to the new tracks that each series runs.

"I think that it's no different coming to a new track; the drivers aren't any different. They are driving as hard as they can to win," Irwin said. "But the higher up you go, people have more respect. Racing clean, you see that more the higher you go up. NASCAR racing, the drivers have a lot of respect for the other drivers out there. So I've learned that. Out on the track, in practice or in a race you're always learning."

Still, Irwin knows every driver in Winston Cup faces high pressure to win.

"Anywhere in Winston Cup there is pressure to win," Irwin said. "Even if you're with a team that's never won, they'll expect things from you."

CHAPTER 11

DALE JARRETT

Jarrett's gel: Finished third in 1998 Winston Cup points standings; winner of 1993 Daytona 500; sat on 1995 Daytona 500 pole; won 1996 Daytona 500 with rookie crew chief Todd Parrott; finished third in the 1996 NASCAR Winston Cup Series standings; won two of four races in the Winston Million in 1996; won 1996 Brickyard 400 at Indianapolis Motor Speedway; career bests with second-place points finish, seven wins, 20 top-fives, and 23 top-10s in 1997; won 1997 races at Bristol and Richmond for first and second short track wins of his NASCAR Winston Cup Series career; led all drivers with 25 top-10 starts in 1997; named the 1997 True Value Man of the Year for his contributions to charitable causes.

Dale Jarrett's father, Ned, is a legend. There's a chance Dale's son, Jason Jarrett, could well be a household name among NASCAR fans in years to come.

But there's no doubt whatsoever that Dale Jarrett is, and will be, a NASCAR legend too.

In 1997, Jarrett set career-high marks with seven wins, 20 top-fives and 23 top-10s. The driver of Robert Yates' No. 88 fell just short of a first NASCAR Winston Cup Series title, but his second-place finish in the standings was a career best as well.

With a new teammate in 1998, Jarrett continued to stay at the top, battling his way to third place in points behind first-place Jeff Gordon and second-place Mark Martin. Ernie Irvan was in the Skittles No. 36 Pontiac as rookie Kenny Irwin, the NASCAR Craftsman Truck Series Cintas Rookie of the Year, took over as Jarrett's team in the Texaco Havoline No. 28.

The transition from Irvan to Irwin—seasoned veteran to hot rookie—was something that took some time for Jarrett to adjust to.

"The one thing a veteran like Ernie Irvan did well with me was communicate," said Jarrett, who was born on Nov. 26, 1956. "I think Kenny is going to be one of the great stars of the future of Winston Cup racing. He's a great kid; he's got a lot of desire."

Although Jarrett is definitely among the senior members of the Winston Cup Series, he believes in staying up with the times. And that involves having a teammate.

"I believe it's a definite advantage," Jarrett said. "There are a lot of opportunities with a two-car operation that are difficult to have in a single-car team. It goes way beyond the testing factor; it allows us to be able to afford a lesser number of people per team and get the job done. We've reduced the cost per team, which in turn is doing it cheaper for our sponsors. That is one of the big advantages, of course, along with the information we share from team to team."

The racing roots in Jarrett's life were established long ago.

"I was pretty young when my dad was racing in the early '60s," Jarrett said. "I always thought it was something I wanted to do, but I was 20 years old before I had the opportunity to get in a stock car. I had raced go-karts before but most of my time was spent in other sports, mostly on the golf course. But since I got in that car at Hickory, I knew that was going to be my focus for the next 20 years. And I've just tried to become a better driver each and every year."

Jarrett started racing in 1977 in the Limited Sportsman Division at Hickory Motor Speedway where Ned was, at one time, the track promoter. Dale's initial NASCAR Winston Cup Series win came in his 129th start at the 1991 Champion 400 at Michigan Speedway in a Wood Brothers car.

But the win that launched his career came in 1993 with Joe Gibbs Racing in the Daytona 500. That season he finished fourth overall in series points. In 1996, Jarrett was third in the points race.

While Ned has a successful career on television as a race announcer and a host of a NASCAR television program, it does not affect Jarrett on the track one bit.

"With all due respect to my dad, because I certainly respect what he does, once I'm in the car. I forget he's there doing his job because I'm so focused on my job," Jarrett said. "It doesn't create any problems for me. It may create some problems for fans who have some problems with him being a little biased toward his son. But he's a professional who tries to be as unbiased as he can to his son when he's doing his job."

NASCAR has changed quite a bit from Ned's era to Dale's. And it is the fastest growing sport in America, something Jarrett credits the France family (NASCAR's founders) with handling very well.

"I believe the France family has done a tremendous job of getting our sport to the point it's at today," Jarrett said. "They seem to have a real good idea of what it takes to get our sport to grow and not to lose what has made it popular in the last 25 years, and more recently, in the last five years. I don't see us taking the turn and hurting ourselves by changing the things that fans have grown to love about Winston Cup and NASCAR racing. Even though we are going into new areas with new speedways, I feel it will enhance our sport even more without losing the roots of the sport."

One thing Jarrett does—like Mark Martin and Jeff Burton, among others—is run the Busch Grand National event when it is at the same track that the Winston Cup race is on a given weekend.

"I feel there is an advantage to running both races," Jarrett said. "We learn something at each and every Busch race I run where there has been a companion event. There are things we can learn about the racetrack and the tires with the Busch car that will be an advantage to the Winston Cup car."

Fan support is high for NASCAR—and for Dale Jarrett, too.

"It's always encouraging as an athlete to have the support of the people who watch and enjoy the things you're doing," Jarrett said. "I think that does almost as much for my confidence, as having the confidence of my crew. I think the fans aspect is as important an aspect as there is in the sport for all of us, from the sponsors to the crews and the drivers who get their recognition nationwide."

NASCAR's growth meant trying—and succeeding in—new markets. "Everyone in NASCAR Winston Cup racing is very excited about the new opportunities," Jarrett said. "The Texas and California markets are areas we want to be involved in. So it will only enhance the popularity and awareness of NASCAR Winston Cup racing."

Jarrett knows he has to be in good physical shape to endure the demands of the long NASCAR season, especially since he runs on the Busch Grand National circuit as well.

"As far as the physical part, I probably train more in the off-season than I do during the season," he said. "It's more cardio-vascular, just running and sit-ups and push-ups. I think just finishing races keeps me in shape. To help me combat the heat, I don't use the air conditioner when I'm driving my personal vehicle, and I rarely roll down the windows. My wife and kids don't appreciate it, but it helps prepare me for Sundays. Just having a car I know can win helps me mentally. And one thing that attracted me to this sport in the first place was the incredible competition level here. It's not hard to get pumped up to go and compete against guys like Jeff Gordon, Dale Earnhardt, Rusty Wallace and Mark Martin."

Jarrett still has plenty of driving ahead of him. When he gets out from behind the wheel a final time, though, he won't be a crew chief. One thing he will do is work on his golf game.

"I don't think I'm going to get into the crew chief business, but I may look into being a team owner at that time," Jarrett said. "I haven't given retirement an exact time frame. I would say that I'm going to go at least 10 more years, I hope. I want to do it until I feel

I can't be competitive anymore because that's what drives me, the competition. If I'm still competitive in 10 years and can go another two or three, then I might do that. As far as being an announcer, I don't know if I'd go in that direction, but being a team owner is something to think about. I know I want to stay involved in the sport. I will certainly look to stay involved in some way, hopefully with Ford Motor Company. And, yes, I do hope to make up for some lost time on the golf course."

Although he lists golf as a hobby, he also lists his family, something that can't be overrated to the family-oriented Dale Jarrett, who credits his wife, Kelly, with helping steer his personal life in the right direction.

"Kelly came along at a time where you could say I needed direction in my life," Jarrett said. "She has helped in a lot of ways. Not only is she my wife but my best friend. It's great to have someone you can count on and enjoy sharing things with, from the times when you are struggling and working hard to make it to the times when you become more successful. There's not much time these days other than at the racetrack. I still enjoy golf. I don't get as many opportunities to play as I used to and I'm not as good as I was, but I still like it. I spend time with my family, mostly. That's what's important."

While the restrictor plates have placed a harness on the top speed potential on the Winston Cup Series, it increased the safety factor for the drivers.

"It is, I guess, maybe a necessity for us," Jarrett said. "If we didn't have them now, we'd be in excess of 220 mph, and that's probably not very safe, even though the cars are extremely safe. The danger is a car getting airborne and into the grandstand, and that's something we'd never want to see. Things are a little tight on the track. Now, when we have so many cars running together, it creates a pretty big wreck when one thing happens. But although I've been pretty successful with the restrictor plate, I feel we can have a good race for the fans without having 30 or 35 cars in one pack."

The need to go faster than 225 miles an hour is no longer there for Jarrett.

"Not anymore—not at 41 years old," Jarrett said. "I've gotten over the thrill of having to go that fast. I think it's the competition that drives me more now. You know, when I was in my late 20s, early 30s, yeah, that was something that really intrigued me, going that fast. But not anymore. I've got four kids, a good wife and a good ride here. I'll just be satisfied with the speeds that we do."

One of Jarrett's closest friends is his crew chief, Todd Parrott.

"I think our relationship has to be stronger than anyone's on the team, or it would be hard for everybody to stay in line," Parrott said. "Off the track, we're good friends, too. I've known Dale since I was a little boy, even though he was a little older. We came from the same family background; our families were both in racing, we both had real bright futures in golf in high school. He's a people person, very honest. He's very sentimental; he means what he says when he tells the guys they've done a great job. He's never down, and you can't get down in this sport. We're alike that way; we both know there are good days and bad days, and we cherish the good days."

Jarrett holds Parrott in the same regard.

"I think that it started out as a business relationship, but it has evolved into a very strong friendship," Jarrett said. "We both have a level of competitiveness inside us that makes us want to be the best in our business of NASCAR Winston Cup racing. That friendship allows us to go with this a little differently than a lot of others because we enjoy being around each other and talking about what we need to do and what we need to accomplish. I think our friendship allows our success to come a little more easily."

At Newton-Conover High in the early 1970s, Jarrett excelled at golf, baseball and football. He was the quarterback on an 8-2 conference championship team during his senior season and was voted the school's Athlete of the Year in 1975.

Golf is more than a hobby to Jarrett. It was almost a way of life for him. Whenever he goes golfing now, his playing partners expect him to shoot par.

"I can't get a good bet," said Jarrett, who was the North Carolina High School Southern District Seven Golfer of the Year in 1974 and '75. "They remember how I used to play, not how I play now. I think we all could do things better when we were younger, and I was able to do pretty well during that part of my life. But they don't forget those days, so they are looking to get back even."

The chance of making a career out of golf is something Jarrett gave a lot of thought to early on.

"I thought about golf a lot," Jarrett said. "But I don't know that I had enough ability to carry it on, to maybe play on the PGA Tour. But I felt for the longest time that I could be involved in golf in some way or another, struggling or trying to make it as a club pro.

"I was a scratch golfer for a good number of years, but not anywhere close to being ready for the PGA Tour," Jarrett said. "Maybe with a number of years of hard work and practice, like I have put into racing, maybe then I could have made it."

While the sports of golf and auto racing appear to be completely opposite, Jarrett sees it differently.

"There are a lot of similarities there," Jarrett said. "I think a golfer is a lot like a race car driver. I'm ready to get in the driver's seat and get away from everything else. Things are in my hands there. My style of golf would carry over to racing too. I have always thrived on competition. Golf is a lot like racing. Just as you think you've started to become pretty good, it brings you back down to earth in a hurry. Golf is a very difficult game. And if things are difficult, I seem to enjoy it more and put a little more effort into it. It takes a level of concentration to do well and be at the top. I still enjoy playing golf. It's just more difficult now because I can't play to the level to which I know I am capable. I look forward to the day I have time to go to the golf course and get some of my skills back."

He even sees similarities in strategy.

"You certainly see it in a lot of other sports where the team or the individual that is ahead is playing not to lose instead of playing to win," Jarrett said. "Even in my days as a golfer, when leading a tournament, I've always found it much more difficult having a three-

or four-stroke lead because you tend to get tentative. You see it in the NFL all the time. You've got to be careful because there's a fine line there."

Jarrett's dad, Ned, knew his son was destined to become a race car driver.

"When I retired, Dale was only about 9 years old," Ned said. "He had been around the sport a lot. Even when the others didn't go, Dale would go with me and ask a lot of questions. He showed some interest in the sport at an early age. Dale came to me and said he thought a couple of his buddies would let him drive their race car if he could come up with an engine. He told me he'd really like to give it a try. We tried to steer him towards a golf career. We thought he would someday make it on the PGA tour. I believe had he put as much effort into golf as he did racing he would have made it in the PGA. I didn't know how tough it was to make it in golf, but I knew how tough it was to make it in racing. I knew the sacrifices he was going to have to make to be successful."

While his performance in 1998 was nothing to overlook, Jarrett really felt like the 1997 season was a big success for himself and his team.

"We accomplished a lot of things that we set out to accomplish," Jarrett said. "We wanted to run up front all the time, and I think we have shown this year that we have done that. Except for a few cases, we've been able to run in the top five or top 10 pretty much every race, so we've accomplished a lot. It's been a very, very satisfying year as far as the things we've been able to accomplish."

It seems to many that Dale Jarrett has had more than his share of bad breaks—from not being able to avoid accidents to fuel mileage woes; it was at the Brickyard 400 in 1998 that Jarrett ran out of gas, which dashed his hopes for another win there. But Jarrett doesn't view misfortunes that way.

"You just hope those things don't happen," he said. "But there have been other times when we probably should have been in a wreck that we were right in the middle of and got out of it. So I just can't look back and say, 'What if' that much because of all the good things that have happened."

CHAPTER 12

BOBBY LABONTE

Labonte's ledger: Finished sixth in 1998 Winston Cup points standings; raced to the 1987 Late Model Stock championship the first time he ran for the points title; won the 1991 NASCAR Busch Series Grand National Division championship; claimed his first career NASCAR Winston Cup Series victory in the 1995 Coca-Cola 600 at Charlotte Motor Speedway; won the 1996 NAPA 500 at Atlanta Motor Speedway as his brother, Terry, clinched the NASCAR Winston Cup Series championship; won NAPA 500 for second consecutive season in 1997; finished seventh in 1997 NASCAR Winston Cup Series standings.

In 1997, Bobby Labonte finished a career-best seventh in the final Winston Cup points standings, despite the fact that he switched to a Pontiac in the off-season. Boosted by back-to-back second places in October stops at Charlotte and Talladega, Labonte did that one better, winning the final race of the season, the NAPA 500 at Atlanta.

Ironically, the win was Labonte's second consecutive NAPA

500, and the 1997 win marked the second year in a row that Labonte's only win of the season came in the last race.

Labonte's first Winston Cup win was at the Coca-Cola 600 at Charlotte in 1995. In that same season, Labonte won both races at Michigan.

Not that Labonte, the younger brother of 1996 Winston Cup points champion Terry Labonte, is a stranger to winning. Bobby Labonte won the Busch Grand National championship in 1991. The following year, he was edged by Joe Nemechek by only three points for the 1992 points championship.

Labonte started racing as a little guy.

"I was four-and-a-half when I got in a little car," Labonte said. "I didn't start really racing until I was 5, but I was out in a parking lot racing my guts out. Between 5 and 10, I went to Baylance, California; Portland, Oregon; Denver, Colorado; Tulsa, Oklahoma; and Columbus, Ohio—all around the country. That was the nationals once a year. Usually, every weekend we'd travel to San Antonio, which is an hour away from Corpus Christi. Then we'd go to Tulsa maybe once a month. Of course, that's 10 hours away. We'd get the pickup truck and the camper and hitch a trailer to it. Terry had two quarter-midgets, and I had two cars on top of those. We ran two classes. I drove one car in each. At one time, there were like 13 classes at San Antonio. I mean, there were junior midgets, light, heavy, stock light, Double A, on up to 13 classes. We held the track record for 12 of them. We didn't run the other one. Finally, after five years they erased all the records and started over. We were the 'Dukes of Corpus.'

"I started racing quarter-midgets, and we raced all over the country," Labonte said. "We started racing stock cars. He'd take a lunch box to work, and he'd come back with a little bit of race car. I really didn't run on any racetracks in Corpus because there weren't any, and we moved when I was 15. When we moved to North Carolina, I ran Caraway, Orange County and South Boston.

"I ran Darlington one time in a Baby Grand car in 1980 or '81," Labonte said, "and Davey Allison started right beside me. He hadn't gotten anywhere yet at that time, either. He was just starting out. Guess you could call us the 'Peachfuzz Gang' back then. I raced a Late Model sportsman at Caraway against Earnhardt, Sam Ard, Jimmy Hensley and Gene Glover, Tony's dad. Gene was national champion in '81 or '82.

"I ran a couple of times at the old Texas World Speedway," said Labonte, a native of Corpus Christi, Texas, who was born on May 8, 1964. "I was running a Chevrolet Malibu and Bobby Allison walked by and said, 'This is a sportsman car?' I got wrecked in the race. I went back to Texas a second time and took Terry's Firebird and qualified second. Bobby (Allison) was first. The rear end broke, and I didn't finish that race. In 1986 is when I finally started racing week in and week out."

Labonte's career took off decades ago when he started racing quarter-midgets in 1969. He moved up to go-karts in 1978.

"I think racing quarter-midgets helps you grow, or anything you race when you're young," Labonte said. "It helps you enjoy the sport and be competitive. Even though those are different kinds of cars, you still learn the aspects of competition. I think it's helped a lot. I was racing them for many years, from when I was 4 to when I was 11 or 12. It's something I will never forget, it's great tutoring to be able to race week in and week out like that all over the country. After that was go-karts, then Late Model competition."

In 1987, Labonte won a Late Model Stocks Championship at Caraway Speedway. He also has a Late Model Sportsman championship. In 1990, Labonte made his debut in the Busch Grand National Series, a circuit in which he now owns a car.

While Busch Grand National provides good training for Winston Cup hopefuls, there are differences going from Busch to Winston Cup.

"I guess it's kind of tough in a way," Labonte said, "because it's not the same, but it's the closest there is."

But don't think Labonte is planning to have a car on the Winston Cup Series.

"On the Winston Cup schedule, about three years ago I would

have said, 'Yeah,'" Labonte said. "But now I would say I'm further away from it. The way the sport is going, I don't want to have to have three or four teams."

Joe Gibbs, the one-time Super Bowl-winning coach for the Washington Redskins, is a good owner to work for, according to Labonte.

"It's more on the business end of it, as he's really busy," Labonte said. "But he spends a lot of time at the race shop. When I go down there, he's usually there. It's a real business relationship, but I always feel like I can talk to him about anything. And I think he can, too. But it's pretty business-wise, as far as wanting to win races."

Labonte still finds time to spend at the shop each week.

"Usually I go to Joe Gibbs Racing at least one day a week, sometimes two," Labonte said. "I go to my Busch shop one or two of the other days before we leave on Thursday to go to the race. And that's if I don't have sponsor commitments to go to out of town."

Along with Gibbs, Labonte has spent a lot of time with a very good crew chief, Jimmy Makar.

"I've been very fortunate to have been with great people and great sponsors for my short career, even though it seems like I have been doing this for quite some time," Labonte said. "But I worked a long time to get here, and now I'm just fortunate to be with Joe Gibbs and Jimmy Makar; they've made it go a lot quicker in terms of advancement than it might have been."

The switch to night racing at more venues is something Labonte—like the fans—seems to be excited about.

"I just think the night racing makes it more exciting," Labonte said. "You're under the lights, sparks are flying, there's cooler weather—it just makes it more exciting, I think."

Labonte will welcome open-wheel and Busch driver Tony Stewart to Gibbs' team next year after being a solo car in a sport dominated by multi-car teams in the late '90s.

"We're looking forward to having a teammate next year," Labonte said. "We're hopeful that it will make our efforts a little bit better, both through the finances and the help of a second team. So, yeah, I'm looking forward to it."

Stewart will get the same treatment Labonte does, and vice versa. It will be, in other words, a team effort the whole way.

"I talked to Joe and Jimmy, and I said if we go to two Winston Cup cars, we don't want an A team and a B team," Labonte said. "We want two A teams. I want to make sure Tony doesn't just help out the 18 car. That's not right, and I don't think he's going to do that. I'll see something in him that will help me, and that's going to help a lot, too. That's going to drive me a little further, and hopefully, the same thing will happen to him."

Some fans wonder if being compared to his brother, Terry, makes Labonte mad at times. Just the opposite is the case.

"That's not a bad person to be compared to," Labonte said. "I'm pretty proud. If I can be compared to him, then I know I'm doing the right thing. We're pretty close. I can't say that we have rivaled each other on or off the track on anything."

And Labonte can give you a bunch of memories that he has of watching Terry drive. "I remember the first time Terry ran Darlington. He was driving a '73 Monte Carlo," Labonte said. "Somebody pushed him to a gas station because he ran out of gas. My mom and dad gave him enough money to stay an extra night. Now we're sleeping in $750,000 buses. I haven't changed the oil in my car since I was 17 years old because I don't drive them long enough anymore. You get free cars to drive and you don't appreciate it as much, but you would miss them if they weren't there. I guess you could say we're spoiled now."

After a big weekend, Labonte sits down and sees where he can improve, grabbing a tape of the race and watching it.

"I usually do that every Sunday night or Monday night," Labonte said. "My father tapes them for me. I usually watch in fast forward. There's usually something you want to see, something you've got on your mind."

One of the highlights of his career is that Labonte has been able to meet a lot of good folks and make some lifelong friends.

"Probably Kenny Wallace and David Green are two of my best friends," Labonte said. "You're friends with everybody but those two are the closest I've known through the years. I can trust them on anything."

When Labonte won in Atlanta in 1996, the fans were treated to something special as Terry drove around the track with Bobby during his victory lap—Terry had clinched the points championship while Bobby won the race. It was Labonte heaven, and the fans responded with a thundering, sustained ovation.

"Oh, that was pretty neat. I didn't think about doing that until the last minute, a kind of a spur of the moment thing," Labonte said. "It was very special—hard to top that one."

"I'd like to congratulate my brother," Terry said at the time. "It was a great day for him."

To win the race, Labonte had to make a brave move on lap 281, going low alongside Jeff Gordon coming out of Turn 4 and making a gutsy three-wide pass into Turn 1 to take over third place.

"That pass made it," Labonte said. "It was three-wide in Turn 1, but I just had to get by Jeff because track position was so important. And I knew Jeff was the one to beat. Making the pass the way I did isn't normal for me, but we were on a mission, and I had to do what I had to do."

And guess who Labonte's racing hero is?

"Probably my dad and Terry," Labonte said. "I watched Terry race for years, I just kind of wanted to be like him."

Labonte is grateful that his parents sacrificed so much to make his and Terry's racing careers a reality.

"He and my mom devoted their whole lives to Terry's and my racing," Labonte said. "As far as time and money, they scraped it all up for us."

Although the Labontes get a lot of their competitiveness from their father, their mother's influence on them can't be overlooked.

"Dad influenced us in a lot of ways, but we get some of it from our mom, too," Labonte said. "Dad worked at a naval station in Texas while we were growing up. He was born and raised in Maine, and when he was 16, he got the heck out of there. It was way too cold. He went to Texas, met my mom, and got married. He started working at the naval air station and eventually retired with a disability. He wrote a lot of technical manuals when he worked there."

When asked about the differences in tracks and how they affect the drivers, Labonte said that the big tracks take more of a mental toll on the drivers than physical. "Some tracks are more physical than others," Labonte said, "while some, like Daytona or Talladega, drain you more mentally."

Bristol is no walk in the park. The short track usually has several accidents play out each race.

"That's probably one of the toughest," Labonte said. "That and Dover are probably two of the most demanding tracks and two of the toughest as far as there not being much room for error."

Like other drivers, Labonte can't single out a favorite track, but he does have a few that stick in his mind.

"Michigan has probably been one of my favorites over the past two or three years. I don't dislike any, even Bristol, as tough as it is and all, I probably should," Labonte said. "I think you have to like them all to be able to run them."

His crew chief knows what Labonte likes—speed.

"Bobby tends to like high speed racetracks," Makar said, "especially places that take some driving skill to get around. It seems to me his better tracks are when he goes to Atlanta, Charlotte, Michigan. Places like that are real, real fast. He tends to do real well at those kind of places. I really think he'll do well down there."

Just competing each week during the season, and adding in a few Busch Grand National races as well, and Labonte has his workout for the week.

"Basically, throughout the racing season, racing week in and week out, you get exercise just driving," Labonte said. "In the off-season is when you really need to exercise."

Like others, Labonte doesn't expect NASCAR's amazing growth to stop, either.

"I guess we'll probably see bigger audiences, more television coverage off the track," Labonte said. "During the week, we'll see more live shows, stuff like that—and possibly more prime time racing in the future, and not necessarily on a Saturday night."

What if Labonte's son wants to race? "When he grows up, I want him to do whatever he wants to do," Labonte said. "If he wants to drive I'll support him. If he wants to play golf or tennis, or if he wants to do nothing, I'll probably support him."

Keeping focus against the top drivers in the world isn't a problem for Labonte. It's something he believes makes him better.

"I think sizing up the competition is one thing, you just try to get focused each day," Labonte said. "You gain confidence trying to outrun them."

Makar was also the crew chief for Rusty Wallace during two of Wallace's wins.

"Just listen to our radio conversations during our race. In general, Bobby Labonte is very calm," Makar said. "But, like anyone, he's got things that get him riled up, although they're few and far between. That is one of his strong points, that he can stay calm instead of getting excited. You need to have that ability."

While qualifying is important, Labonte sets a modest goal for where he needs to start a race.

"Our goal is to always qualify in the top 25," Labonte said.

NASCAR's oldest speedway—Darlington—is also its most challenging.

"The first time I drove Darlington was in an old Daytona Dash car," Labonte said. "Darlington isn't wide enough for two of those little cars running side by side, much less big Winston Cup cars. But I've always liked Darlington. I've always respected it, and I was taught to do that by my brother, Terry, and other people. Everybody told me I should be twice as serious as normal about driving around this place because it will get you."

The Texas native also found the Texas Speedway to be unique.

"It's a unique racetrack," Labonte said. "It's not like Charlotte. It's not like Atlanta. It's not like Michigan. It's not like Richmond. It's not like any other track."

As for the races themselves, it's hard to beat Daytona, but the Brickyard comes close.

"The Daytona 500 is still the biggest race because of its history," Labonte said. "I'd rank the Brickyard second, a close second. That's just because of all its tradition. It's the biggest race as far as prestige, other than Daytona. You can just tell by all the preparation all the teams put into it. Most of the teams test there, usually they build a new car to run up there, and just generally put more effort into it. But what you've got to watch is not letting yourself get caught up in the hype. You can't lose sight of the big picture. The Brickyard 400 is what you want to make out of it. It's big, but when you really think about it, it's just another racetrack we go to. Once you get there, it still boils down to the same thing. You have to do all the same things in preparing for this race as any other if you want to be a contender to win."

In 1998, Labonte fared well at Daytona, but got little notice since it was Dale Earnhardt's first career win at Daytona.

"I don't think anybody knows we finished second at Daytona," Labonte said. "But I do. I was the first one to see Dale win it. We definitely remember it. I would have ended up in the pond (the infield water, Lake Lloyd). I really had a head of steam, and then I got to Dale's bumper, and I was trying to figure out what to do. By the time I was going to make a move, the caution came out. I learned a lot up to that point, and I don't know if I could have gone any further anyway. I know he was worried about us, and I was wanting to get by him, but it was going to be hard to do. Like I said, I probably would have ended up in the pond."

The only thing Labonte dislikes more than losing is letting a race slip away.

"When you don't capitalize on a chance to win, that makes me mad," Labonte said. "That's because those days don't come very often. When it's there, you've got to take advantage of it."

That attitude was shown in August 1998, when Labonte was runner-up to Jeff Gordon at the Michigan Speedway in the Pepsi 400.

"I've never," Labonte said, "been so disappointed with second."

Losing is costly in three ways: points, pride and pockets (money).

"Not only does winning pay a lot more, it just means a lot," Labonte said. "When you finish second three times, it's like nobody quite remembers that."

Consistency is the key.

"Every team is going to have a poor finish or two," Labonte said. "What separates the championship contenders is bouncing back from the bad finishes."

CHAPTER 13

KEVIN LEPAGE

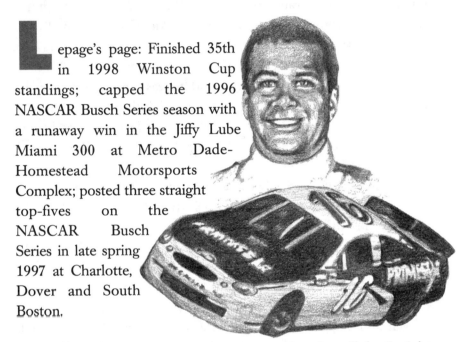

L epage's page: Finished 35th in 1998 Winston Cup standings; capped the 1996 NASCAR Busch Series season with a runaway win in the Jiffy Lube Miami 300 at Metro Dade-Homestead Motorsports Complex; posted three straight top-fives on the NASCAR Busch Series in late spring 1997 at Charlotte, Dover and South Boston.

In a lot of ways, Kevin Lepage represents not just all that is right with NASCAR, but all that is right with sports—and life—in general.

He didn't always have the most money. He didn't always have the best equipment. But no one ever had more heart, and now he's been rewarded, joining one of the top teams in the history of NASCAR, Jack Roush's Winston Cup Series group.

Lepage knew his destiny was in racing. In fact, he felt his first passion for racing at a very—VERY—young age. Lepage was born on June 26, 1962, and lives in Vermont with his wife and children.

"Since I was 2 years old sitting in my dad's dragster seat," Lepage said. "I knew right there that I wanted to be a race car driver.

I just had to have the breaks and/or the finances to do it, and through my career it seems one or the other has always been there."

Lepage began his career in 1980 on short tracks in Vermont before competing on the American-Canadian Tour.

"I started in 1980 in Vermont driving a Busch North car," Lepage said. "My brother had been in the cars five years prior. The first time out I won my heat race and finished 10th, and so I pretty much replaced my brother right there. I was Rookie of the Year in 1980. It was a car owned by my dad. My dad used to drag race years ago. Then my brother started Busch North racing. In 1980 I was supposed to race the weekly series, and he was supposed to tour. But in the first race I won my heat and finished 10th overall and pretty much secured my ride for the rest of the year. From that point on I had set a goal to get to NASCAR racing. I always wanted to become a Busch and Winston Cup driver. I concentrated on doing everything I could to do that. You've got to understand everything, not just how to drive, but the off-track stuff like talking to fans, the sponsors and the media."

Lepage said anyone can get into racing, but they have to be willing to pay their dues.

"Probably the best thing to do is to start at a local racetrack with a local race team," Lepage said. "Then work your way up to Busch or Winston Cup. You have to start at the bottom. A lot of people want to jump right in, but we don't have time to train you. You have to show your experience and move on up."

The Busch North Series proved to be a good training ground for Lepage.

One of Lepage's toughest foes in the Busch North Series ended up being more than just a mentor to Lepage—John Paul Cabana.

"He had several years of experience when I arrived on the scene. He was always there every week when I first got there," Lepage said. "But to be honest with you, I really enjoyed racing against him, in fact, so much so that I asked him to be one of the best men in my wedding a few years back. He was there for me when I first got in the racing game, and he was there for me when I started maturing with the sport. He was one I looked up to."

While Lepage enjoyed racing in the Busch North Series, he claimed the step up to Busch Grand National was a logical one.

"The first reason why I left was my wife and I decided that we'd done everything in the North except win a championship," Lepage said. "When we came South, the transition was pretty easy. I think having the sponsorship of Vermont Teddy Bear really helped because everybody asked about it."

Lepage said the jump from Busch Grand National North Series to the big-time Busch Grand National Series was exciting.

"The biggest difficulty I had was getting used to radial tires and bigger racetracks," Lepage said.

He also thinks there will be many other drivers making a similar series jump in years to come. "I do believe NASCAR North is a stepping stone to the Busch Series," Lepage said.

After riding at Bear Ridge and ThunderRoad, Lepage had to get used to a higher level of competition in the Busch Grand National Series.

"The competition differs because here in the Busch Series every week we have 40 champions. They were all champions in some form or fashion where they came from," Lepage said. "At ThunderRoad we have drivers who are experienced and good drivers, but they are not like the guys who run every week on the Busch Series. Great places to drive though—both those facilities."

Still, he won't forget his racing heritage.

"I do love short track racing—it's the only thing I did for 13 years," Lepage said. "But now that I'm down here in the South I love racing the mile-and-a-half and the superspeedway tracks."

While he no longer runs Busch North races, he still thinks about the tracks.

"Actually I have two favorites up there," Lepage said, "but the one that really relates is Catamount Stadium in Vermont. It's no longer around, though, which is too bad. It's an industrial park now.

But Myrtle Beach and South Boston have a lot of similarities to it—that's probably why I run so well there."

A native of Vermont, Lepage is proud that other New England natives, including Steve Park and Ricky Craven, have made names of their own in NASCAR.

"Obviously, there are a lot of northerners venturing South," Lepage said. "It's just getting in the right place, under the right circumstances. You don't need to be a northerner—you just need to be in the right situation down here in the South. There are talented drivers everywhere."

In 1994, he moved on to NASCAR's Busch Grand National Series. In 1994 and 1995, Lepage owned his fifth Busch Grand National team.

Like several other drivers, Lepage spent time as an owner. It gave him a different perspective, and had both advantages and disadvantages.

"Owning my own race team gave me a different perspective of the sport, both the business aspect and the racing aspect," Lepage said. "Now that it's just the racing part, it's taken a lot of pressure off both my brain and my wallet. There are some days I wish I was an owner again, but it's best that I just focus on what I do best, and that's work as a driver."

The hardest part of trying his hand as an owner was mostly financial.

"Actually, just working with the reservations, hotels, rental cars and per diems—just a lot of strain over things like that, and the bills," Lepage said. "I'm sure you can see the improvement since I've no longer got those extra responsibilities."

After struggling for a while, Lepage joined Ridling in 1996. Lepage did not let the sponsor woes plague him—he was one of only 11 drivers to make each of the first 11 races in 1996, leading to a meeting with David Ridling, who had gained an appreciation of Lepage's perseverance.

While some fans—and even those within the racing ranks—might wonder if it is fair for established Winston Cup drivers to also drive semi-regularly in the Busch Grand National Series, Lepage welcomes the challenge.

"No, I don't mind. Charlotte is a perfect example. We were running fourth with Cup guys ahead and behind me," Lepage said. "When you can go right with those guys, it does nothing but good things for your team and your confidence. It's all part of becoming a better driver, a winning driver. So I like running with those guys. I hope they never go away. I had that talk with Jeff Burton at Dover. When you beat 'em and race against them, it lets them know what kind of driver you are. And when you do make that move (up to Winston Cup), it just makes it easier."

Anyone interested in getting into racing can learn from Lepage, who knows what it takes to get into—and stay in—the sport.

"First of all, you need to go in with a positive attitude," said Lepage. "Because there are more downs than ups, listen to everything people have to say. They're not always right, but you should listen. And be patient because you must first finish before you can finish first."

Lepage ran up front most of the season, and ended 1996 with his first career win in the Jiffy Lube 300 at Miami-Dade.

His win at Homestead in the Jiffy Lube 300 during the 1996 season was quite a boost for Lepage.

"The win did more mentally than it did anything else," Lepage said. "There are a lot of guys in the Busch Series that never get to Victory Lane. And to get to Victory Lane on CBS against the Winston Cup boys on a mile-and-a-half track really did a lot for me."

Lepage just edged Bobby Labonte and Mark Martin for the win.

"I knew when Mark and Bobby began racing each other so hard, that would help me out," Lepage said. "I decided to run my own line and I got around them and then we just pulled away from them."

It's a memory Lepage recalls with a smile.

"It was a very special day in my career," Lepage said. "So many drivers come down here and try to be successful in Busch and Winston Cup. It was just one of them days. The car, the team, the pit calls, the yellow flags, they all fell my way. We raced at a tri-oval like that before, and you really had to have everything right for that…I think I was beating a lot of people because of that."

In 1997, Lepage ran with LJ racing on the Winston Cup Tour. Lepage drove in 1998 for Doug Taylor's Channellock Chevy and then left LJ Racing's Winston Cup ride when one of the premier owners in the sport, Jack Roush, offered Lepage a ride.

Going from Busch Grand National to Winston Cup was no easy challenge, either.

"The hardest part of the transition is figuring out what the Winston Cup wants compared to the Busch car," Lepage said. "The Winston Cup car has more horsepower and is longer, which means the straightaway speeds are higher. That means you can't take these cars into the corners as hard as the Busch cars—that's probably been the most difficult part in the change."

Despite driving for Little Joe's racing team without a sponsor for much of the first part of the Winston Cup season, Lepage continued to persevere.

"I've always surrounded myself through the years with teams that were under-funded and under-sponsored," Lepage said. "I always seemed to be able to bring 'em to the top. I'm hoping someday Kevin Lepage can surround himself with a high-quality, high-profile race team and actually see what Kevin Lepage is made of. I think I'm a winner. I know I'm a winner. I've done it in the past, but I don't know if I can do it week in and week out until we get the equipment and people to do it with. We want to do this deal. We want to make races and do the best job we can. There's no ego in this organization. Everybody wants to be in Winston Cup. Everybody wants to be successful in Winston Cup. When you've got that want, that burning desire, it just makes you want to work a little extra harder. When you use your time, you use every minute to get the most out of it so you don't waste half your time. Money and personnel are key ingredients in this sport. Most of our practice is on the track when the green flag falls, and that's tough, but we're hanging in there, doing the best we can with what we've got."

That all changed on June 26 during the '98 season when Lepage signed with Roush Racing.

Still, Lepage felt bad about leaving LJ Racing. "With the opportunities that had come along for me, I needed to make sure I did what was right for my wife and me for the future," Lepage said. "Hooking up with Roush Racing is the dream of a lifetime for any number of drivers out there, and I was just fortunate enough to be the one to get the call. I'll tell you, being associated with PRIMESTAR and the Jack Roush team, it's a great opportunity ahead of me. He's surrounded me with a great team, and I think it's going to be a great career move for me. We're real excited about the whole thing."

How Lepage ended up with Roush is a wild ride in its own right. In Dover in late May, according to Lepage, "a lady gave me a business card, and it read, 'Call me Monday morning, urgent.' I called, and Jeff Smith (of Roush Racing) asked me if I wanted to drive for Jack Roush, beginning at Michigan. It didn't take long for me to say yes. It still had to be approved by the PRIMESTAR people, and they were pleased with what they saw (in a meeting at New Hampshire). Then we made the announcement. All of those phone calls happened within a short period of time. I talked to a lot of people, but my wife and I decided that it was an opportunity of a lifetime to be with Jack Roush, so that's what we went with."

Lepage thus took over the No. 16 Primestar Ford that Ted Musgrave had driven up to that point in the season.

"I see some things in Kevin that I think can really turn this program around," Roush said. "Kevin is young and hungry. We have a young, hungry crew chief in James Ince and a group of guys at the shop who know how to put cars together. To me, Kevin is the final piece to the puzzle toward putting that program in Victory Lane."

Lepage said it was an honor to join the modern-day legendary owner.

"It is really hard for me to describe how it feels to have an owner like Jack Roush take notice," Lepage said. "This is the opportunity you work your whole life for, and I'm ready to go out there and prove him right."

Lepage did just that with a 17th-place finish in his August debut at the Pepsi 400. He followed that Aug. 24 with a career-best 10th place finish at the Goody's Headache Powder 500 in Bristol. Even Roush showed emotion after the race.

"Great job!" Roush said as he grabbed Lepage and gave the weary driver a bear hug that just about knocked him down.

"I think I like this place," Lepage said. "It was a pretty good weekend for me here."

That's because he had won the night before, on Aug. 21, 1998, in the wreck-filled Food City 250 Busch Grand National race. Winston Cup regular Dale Jarrett had dominated the race, leading 139 of 250 laps. But his lead was half a lap when a spin brought caution. On the restart, another big accident eliminated the second, third, fifth, eighth and 10th-place cars. After another stop in the action that lasted nearly half an hour and brought out the red flag, Lepage and Phil Parsons closed on Jarrett. Lepage took a run past Jarrett for the title, bringing Parsons with him as Parsons took second and Jarrett was third.

"Dale (Jarrett) was a little tight there coming off the corners," Lepage said. "I got a run on him once, and he came down on me. I knew he was going to do that. I said I'll give it one more chance, and I got a heck of a run coming off Turn 2. This motor ran really well. It pulled us down the backstraight, and we got a chance to get underneath him. The Channellock Chevrolet wasn't good on long runs. I was ready to settle for fourth place. If there had been a caution instead of a red flag, I wouldn't have been able to do it. I knew that if the tires cooled down, my car would be good for five laps."

Lepage said the Winston Cup veterans were very helpful when he first made the transition from Busch Grand National.

"They want you to be comfortable out there," Lepage said. "If you're not—if you're on edge—you could cause problems out there. I ask them for advice, and they're always willing. For instance, I asked Sterling Marlin for some advice about qualifying for Bristol; then I went out and out-qualified him by one spot. I thanked him for the advice. He said, 'Yeah, but you outrun me.' But he was really nice. When I first came down, one of the drivers who first comes to mind is Dale Earnhardt. When I was at New Hampshire, we weren't running well, and Dale came over with some advice and drew a little map on his tool box. That day we picked up three-tenths. Crew chiefs helped a lot, too. Bob Johnson, who works with Randy LaJoie helped me three weeks in a row, and I out-qualified Randy each week, and the fourth week he wouldn't help me again."

One of Lepage's racing legends is a familiar face in the winner's circle.

"My role model in racing would have to be David Pearson," Lepage said. "I always admired the way he drove. He was always there at the end. He never really took any chances that were unnecessary. If he had a seventh-place car, that's where he brought it home. So I guess I model my driving after him. I've always been amazed with the guy. Growing up, I never missed a race on TV with David in it. David Pearson was probably one of my biggest heroes. And when I came down here, I was always amazed at what Alan Kulwicki accomplished as an owner-driver. "

It might seem like some of the Winston Cup drivers dominate week after week, year after year. But Lepage cautions that there are no slouches in the series.

"That's a question I brought up with a couple Winston Cup drivers at Atlanta. I had it in my mind, and they basically said the same, that there are no second-rate Winston Cup teams," Lepage said. "There are just some with more money."

While he is racing against some living NASCAR legends, Lepage is careful to keep his focus—especially since being a Winston Cup/Busch driver requires such a high talent level.

"It's very exciting to race against Dale Earnhardt, Jeff Gordon and Rusty Wallace," Lepage said. "But this is a business, and I try and compete. For the first couple of races last year, I was kind of scared to race with them. But with the respect we've earned this year, it's great to try and go out and race them, pass them, beat them. They're a lot of fun to be around."

A fan offered this question to Lepage: If you were leading on the last lap, who would you least want in your rearview mirror?

"Doesn't make a difference," Lepage said, "as long as I'm far enough ahead of them."

The move to the new tracks and superspeedways, as well as the road courses—all of which seem to seat more fans—is something Lepage doesn't really relish, even though he understands the economics behind the decision.

"I think both series will slowly get away from short tracks," Lepage said, "as much as we don't want to leave them because they are our grass roots. The short tracks just can't put up the money that the series will be needing. It's kind of a shame, but I don't think it will happen real soon. The series will probably get away from the short tracks, but that's just my opinion."

He also supports the new regions that now host NASCAR events.

"NASCAR is growing," Lepage said, "and we need to go to different markets. Going to the new markets of Las Vegas and California, I think, is what is going to make the series bigger and better."

Many drivers profess to like a certain kind of track; Lepage makes a conscious effort to not prefer one over another.

"It doesn't really make a difference," Lepage said. "I seem to enjoy both. If you have a preference, then your mind can play games with you. I just try and get excited for every track we visit."

While the drivers, crews and owners steer the cars around the track, Lepage said it is the fans who steer NASCAR's incredible growth.

"It's been overwhelming on the fan response for NASCAR and me, since I had Vermont Teddy Bear as a sponsor," Lepage said. "I just hope I stay around long enough to get a fan base as big as Dale Earnhardt's because I really enjoy the fans and the things they do and write in. I really enjoy reading them."

While his nickname "Pepe" might conjure up images of a certain not-so-nasal-friendly cartoon skunk, Lepage claims no resemblance exists.

"Pepe is a Frenchman, like I am," Lepage said. "And it's just a nickname I got at Homestead. It's just a nickname."

Lepage had entertained owning a NASCAR Craftsman Truck Series team. However, he no longer sees that direction as feasible.

"Not that I don't want to do it, but this has become more demanding than I wanted it to be," Lepage said. "We're trying to do this Cup deal, and we don't want to spread ourselves too thin. I don't think I could do it unless I just owned the truck team and had somebody drive for me."

CHAPTER 14

DAVE MARCIS

Marcis moments: Runner-up to Richard Petty in 1975 NASCAR Winston Cup championship battle, his best-ever season point finish; Wisconsin short-track champion in 1965; has won in USAC stock car and Late Model (now NASCAR Busch Series) events; has more than 800 starts, the most of any active NASCAR Winston Cup Series driver and second all-time to Richard Petty; qualified for his 30th consecutive Daytona 500 in 1997, the most of any driver; qualified for a fifth-place start in 1997 Miller 500 at Dover; became the eighth driver in NASCAR history to top $1 million in career earnings.

Still going. . .and going. . .how about that Dave Marcis?

Once a short track champion in Wisconsin, Marcis' first NASCAR race was the Dayton 500 in 1968. The first series win was at Martinsville in the 1975 Old Dominion 500—that marked the same year he finished second to Richard Petty for the series title. Since that first series win did not come until his 225th start, don't think Marcis is easily discouraged.

Petty, the "King," still refers to Marcis as one of the top drivers he ever competed against.

"I've always admired Richard," Marcis said. "He was my idol when I was growing up. He was the one I followed racing through *Hot Rod* magazine in the '50s. I had my car painted blue; I was kinda copying Richard. When I first got into NASCAR, Richard was one of the first to come and welcome me aboard. I always watched Richard and would try and do things like him, like accommodating the fans. When I first started, I raced Richard a lot, and I raced him clean. I think there is a lot of respect among drivers when we race at the speeds we do and the way we do it. If you go out there and just knock guys out of the way and just spit them out, they certainly won't have any respect for you."

Another close friend is Richard Childress of Richard Childress Racing, or RCR, and RCR's most notable driver, Dale Earnhardt.

"My relationship with Richard Childress goes back to when Richard drove," Marcis said. "Then when Richard decided to become a car owner, he found there are times when Dale is so busy with sponsorship things that he's not available to do any testing. Richard asked if I could help them test, and I agreed. Dale's comfortable with my testing. I can help them; then Richard helps me with engines for all the restrictor-plate races and his guys help with some chassis and body stuff. It's just been a good relationship for both of us. When Richard raced we were good friends. Neil Bonnett used to test for them; when they lost Neil, I stepped in. I'd done a little testing for them before. But Dale has always been happy with the testing I've done and the adjustments I've made. They've seemed to fit his driving style very well."

Among the many friends Marcis counts in the Winston Cup Series are the "Intimidator" and Jeff Gordon, along with the Rainbow Warrior's crew chief, Ray Evernham.

"I get along good with Dale Earnhardt. Basically, I get along good with all of them," Marcis said. "But Earnhardt and I are pretty good friends. Jeff Gordon, Ray Evernham—Ray worked with us in IROC. Richard Petty has been a good friend. We all pretty much get along good, the drivers, the crew chiefs and all. We travel around the country for 32 weeks or so, and it would be pretty miserable if we didn't get along well."

Testing for Earnhardt also benefits Marcis.

"It helps a lot because they have a Chevrolet Monte Carlo just like I do," Marcis said. "Especially with the aerodynamics and such of Talladega, I can use some of their information."

Marcis enjoys interacting with the drivers, and he never is above offering guidance to the younger ones who seek him out.

"For the most part, I'm always happy to help," Marcis said. "They feel like I have a lot of chassis knowledge, and of course, I've raced on all the tracks for years. A lot of the guys come around wanting to know things to do with the race car, things to make it drive better. That will change some this year with the addition of California and Texas, but still, I've got as much experience as anyone out there. I've worked a lot with Richard Childress and Dale Earnhardt, but I can say that they've helped me a lot, too. I use their engines on restrictor-plate races. Their whole team has helped us. Whenever we've needed help, they all jump in and give us a hand. And partly because of things like that I have as much enthusiasm to win a Winston Cup event as I did 10 years ago or 20 years ago. I love it, I just love racing. It's been my whole life, and I'm always happy to contribute to the people who are trying to do the same thing. It's all for the good of the sport."

Marcis has racing bloodlines that extend back to his father, who owned a garage and wrecking yard at the family's Wisconsin home. Former IMCA driver Ernie Derr, another Wisconsin product, was the first driver Marcis really looked up to.

"I was always around automobiles because my dad owned a wrecking yard and repair shop," Marcis said. "I also had a friend who lived by an old dirt track that we used to go to. I used to be able to take an old car from the wrecking yard and put some roll bars into it and take it to the track in my hometown of Wausau, Wisconsin. I tried racing, and I've liked it ever since. I started at Red Mountain State Park Speedway, a track near my home, with a 1949

Ford. I continued racing stock cars, and when I decided I wanted to race for a living, I looked at all my options. Basically what it boiled down to was, if you wanted to race stock cars for a living, you needed to do it in NASCAR."

Getting into the Winston Cup scene back then meant moving across the country to North Carolina.

"Basically, I just wanted to race. I'd watched racing all my life," Marcis said. "I read *Hot Rod* magazine and kept up with the sport. I looked at the size of the racetracks down here and the size of the racetracks we ran in Wisconsin, and I felt like our times were pretty close. So I figured maybe if I could get down here and get a chance, that I could make it. I just decided to come and try it. So I bought a used race car from someone down here and I gave it a try. I'm still here."

Marcis still makes time to get back to Wisconsin.

"I get up to Wisconsin in the fall of each year," he said. "I try to get up and do a little fishing in the fall, and I get up there for two weeks around Christmastime."

As a test driver for the IROC Series, Marcis keeps his racing skills up to speed.

A link to NASCAR's past showed that he is just fine in the present during the 1998 season.

Marcis overcame several failures to qualify to finish the 1998 season strong. In 1997, Marcis finished 42nd in the points standings.

However, Marcis' legend will forever be linked to footwear—he started wearing wing-tipped shoes to alleviate the burns that many drivers experienced. While some found it funny, Marcis only did it because, quite simply, it worked.

"I wear the wingtips because back in the old days we had a lot of problems burning our feet. And everybody was trying something," Marcis said. "One day at North Wilkesboro, David Pearson asked if I didn't have any shoes with leather soles, and I said just my dress shoes. So I wore them that day and I did not burn my feet, so I've been wearing them ever since."

While the driving is the same, the sport has changed.

"As far as how it's changed, it's so competitive," said Marcis, who has three children with his wife, Helen. "Years ago, you'd see an eight- to nine-mph spread. Now you don't see that, it's more like a two- to three-mph spread. It's so much more competitive and so much tighter."

The cars are also quite different from when Marcis started.

"The cars today are so much more aerodynamic than years ago, so it's pretty hard to compare the car of the past with the car of today," said Marcis. "We didn't have the shock technology or the radial tires that Goodyear has today. Today for qualifying we'll set up springs and shocks for a lot of rebound, but for the race setup, we go through the NASCAR inspection, and they hang a 150 lb. weight on the rear of the car, and it's only allowed to settle three inches. So for that we really have to change our springs and shock setups. The cars have changed a lot since I began, and the biggest change is the aerodynamics. There's been a major change in brakes from running drum brakes to disc brakes. There has also been major changes in shocks. I'd have to credit Alan Kulwicki with that change. He was always working on shocks, and he ran them well. So other people began running them."

One of the factors that has contributed to Marcis' longevity in the sport is the fact that he's worked hard to stay in decent shape.

"I really am an active person. I've always tried to watch my weight," Marcis said, who was born March 1, 1941, and likes to hunt, fish and cook. "I eat good foods; I don't eat a lot of special foods. I don't weight train, but I do stay active. I'm up at six and go to my shop, and I don't get home until eight or nine. It's the same at the tracks. I'm a big eater: I love vegetables, potatoes and beans and when I can, good country food."

Late in the 1998 season, Marcis was preparing for his 31st Daytona 500.

"It wasn't anything that was planned," Marcis said. "I just really enjoy the sport, and my whole life is about NASCAR and Winston

Cup racing. I just don't feel like retiring, and it's how I make my living. I just enjoy the sport. It's my job; it's where I make my living. I just enjoy being here. I look forward to every race every week. I plan on doing that for quite a while yet."

Although Marcis won't talk about a retirement timeline, he knows he will be involved with NASCAR when his driving days are over.

"When I decide to retire from driving, I do plan on staying on as a team owner, but I do not have anybody for my car in mind," he said. "I just love it; I enjoy it. I still enjoy it, and the more competitive it is, the more I enjoy it. I look forward to every year."

Marcis even remembers back when Chrysler was involved in NASCAR. If Chrysler came back, would Marcis get behind the wheel?

"I don't know for sure. I've been with General Motors and the Chevrolets for quite a while," Marcis said. "It depends on what kind of deal it would be. It's one of those deals where you'd never say no. I think Chrysler would be welcomed back into NASCAR. When they were here, as everyone knows, they were very competitive. I think we'd certainly welcome them back. And with the rules today, and Ford turning the four-door Taurus into a hand-built race car, I don't see why Chrysler can't be doing the same thing."

One thing fans notice about Marcis is that he doesn't always choose to pit when the other cars do, especially if there is a chance to get extra points by leading a lap.

"Sometimes, if things are tight in the points, we stay out to try and lead a lap. It means a lot for provisionals," Marcis said. "Hopefully, we can be more competitive and run with the leaders, so we can pit with the leaders. That's what we're aiming for, to get our cars a little more competitive and get a little better pit crew."

Getting competitive also means getting enough financial backing, an opportunity Marcis hopes will present itself for the 1999 season.

"I would drive for a major team if the opportunity presented itself," Marcis said. "I would then probably put someone in my car, so I would still try to run a team here."

Not having similar financial resources is frustrating at times.

"It's tough," Marcis said. "It's my desire to be competitive. I work hard and try to be competitive. We watch what we spend; we make every dollar count. A lot of teams do a lot of R&D work and buy parts that they don't even use on their race car. But we can't afford to do that; we don't waste any money. I've also got support from many small businesses. Small businesses help us out a lot with expenses that I would otherwise have to go out and buy to be competitive in racing."

If his own team were to come up with more financing—like something comparable to what the major teams have—Marcis believes it would really help his position in the points standings.

"We would spend the money on hiring more people, people with more knowledge in certain areas," Marcis said. "We would improve the engine programs, but I feel like our engine program is going fine. We would also like to get some people with more aerodynamics experience."

Although many drivers have pre-race rituals, Marcis just kind of takes care of the basics.

"It's just trying to get a good night's sleep and a good meal—but I try and do that all the time," Marcis said. "I just want to have the car prepared like you want it on Saturday afternoon. And if you're not happy with it, think about how you want to change it. I think most teams do make changes Sunday morning after they think about that last practice on Saturday."

Marcis also showed he's a force to be reckoned with when he qualified fifth at Dover.

"Dover's been a good track over the years for us," Marcis said. "But since it went to concrete it hasn't been as good. We made a lot of changes to our car. We rolled off pretty good, and I think we were one of the fastest cars after the first practice. After we broke for lunch and came back, I think we were in the top 13 or so. So we knew we could run well. I don't know if we expected to qualify fifth, but we certainly expected to get in the top 15."

While Dover has been good to Marcis, he always had a good perspective regardless of the track on the series circuit in a given week.

"You know we've always got high hopes wherever we go," Marcis said. "We always try to keep our spirits up."

Asked to name one highlight from his long, stellar career, Marcis simply can't.

"I don't know, there have been so many of them. I think I just enjoy racing," he said. "Coming from Wisconsin and getting into NASCAR was a great thing. As a boy I got a *Hot Rod* magazine and all I read about was Richard Petty and David Pearson. Winning my first race at Martinsville with Harry Hyde, that I'll never forget. Also winning a race at Richmond when it rained, with a car from our own shop. There's just been so many, it's hard to pick out one."

NASCAR, as an organization, has made almost all the right moves at every turn.

"You know, NASCAR is trying to get the Winston Cup circuit to be as competitive as possible," Marcis said. "It's racing and it's also entertainment. We all have to be thankful, I think, that all of you fellas as well as us, the drivers and the media, the fans are what makes it possible for us to all have a job. And we want to put a good show on for them."

The new tracks in Las Vegas and Texas, among other places, have helped open up NASCAR to new fans.

"Hopefully, with the new tracks being in bigger areas, they're going to increase the revenue that we can take in, so really it should help us," Marcis said. "That's the way I look at that."

It also gives the drivers more exposure to potential sponsors.

"Definitely, it opens up some more markets, and that's what I said, I hope it creates more revenue for us," Marcis said. "It causes a little bit more travel and things like that, but the sport continues to grow and expand, and that's what it's all about if we want to see it succeed like it has."

How tough is Marcis? Well, in 1992 he got tangled up with Darrell Waltrip and Marcis' leg was broken. That did not, however, shelve Marcis.

"I didn't miss any races—I remember that," Marcis said. "I brought Jim Sauter in to help out. I practiced in the car, he practiced in the car, I qualified it and I started the race and Jim got in. I think we did that for three or four events, and then I ran all of them after that. I have five pins and a steel plate in my left leg. They said I could get them taken out if I wanted but they ain't bothered me."

Marcis has also stood unfailingly loyal to his sponsors.

"I guess everybody out there, Unocal, Goodyear, Chevrolet, they've stood by me, and I've stood by them," he said. "I've turned down at least three or four oil sponsorships over the years. They weren't super big, but they were companies that wanted to get into the sport. What they were offering, as far as I was concerned, really wasn't enough to throw away everything that Unocal had done for me over the years. I just believe in standing by people that stand by me, that's all."

To stay near the top of the point standings, a team has to run consistently well.

"I think you've got to get momentum going and carry it from week to week," Marcis said.

Marcis also tested IROCs at Indy, and was one of the first to drive a stock car around the Indianapolis Motor Speedway. So when he was there for the first Brickyard 400, Marcis felt a twinge of pride and emotion.

"It was really a great feeling to come here first with the IROC cars to see how feasible it would be, then to come here with the Winston Cup cars," Marcis said. "That first Brickyard 400, well, I was really tickled to death to run on this speedway. I had interest in Indy cars and listened to every Indianapolis 500 growing up as a little boy in Wisconsin. In our travels during the 1970s and early '80s, anywhere I'd go, people would identify me with racing, and one of the first questions they'd ask was, 'Do you race at Indianapolis?' Of course, I'd have to explain to them I drove stock cars in NASCAR, and the cars at Indy are open-wheel cars, and that stock cars didn't race at Indy. Now when they ask that question, I can say, 'Yes, I race at Indianapolis.'"

CHAPTER 15

JEREMY MAYFIELD

Mayfield's mains: Finished seventh in the 1998 Winston Cup points standings; won Sportsman class at Kentucky Motor Speedway Rookie of Year and Most Improved Driver; competed at Nashville Motor Raceway from 1990 to 1992, had three poles, two wins, 10 top-fives and 14 top-10s to finish fourth in points; ran ARCA Series in 1993, scored eight top-fives and 10 top-10s and won ARCA Rookie of the Year title; streaked to first career Bud Pole at Talladega in 1996; set new personal marks with three top-fives and eight top-10s, as well as 13th-place overall finish in 1997; turned in strong performances at two of circuit's biggest races in 1997 with sixth at Daytona 500 and fifth at Brickyard 400; notched first career Winston Cup win at Pocono 500 in 1998; took NASCAR Winston Cup Series points lead for first time following 1998 California 500 presented by NAPA.

Continual improvement. Those two words sum up the career of Jeremy Mayfield. Although he turned just 29 years old in May of 1998, Mayfield already had four years of Winston Cup experience under his belt. Remarkably, in all of those years, he improved from 37th place in 1994 to 31st the following year, 26th the next and then

13th place in the point standings in 1997. Mayfield has excelled on almost every track.

When Mayfield was 14, he started racing go-karts in Owensboro, Kentucky. He did it for five years before stepping up to the Sportsman Class at the Kentucky Motor Speedway where, in his first season, he claimed Rookie of the Year and Most Improved Driver Awards. A year later, Mayfield moved to Late Models where he entered 11 races and won seven.

The native of Owensboro—one of the half-dozen O'Boys from the racing-rich town on the Ohio River—Mayfield won the ARCA Rookie of the Year in 1993.

"I guess it was the ARCA series that was my first professional race," Mayfield said. "I think I was 20 years old. That was at Atlanta Motor Speedway. My first Winston Cup race was Charlotte Motor Speedway, and I was 23 years old when I ran there."

In 1998 Mayfield had another first—his first Winston Cup victory, winning at Pocono. His childhood hero—fellow Owensboro native and two-time Winston Cup points champion Darrell Waltrip—was one of the drivers Mayfield had to pass to pick up his first Winston Cup win, where he led five different times for a total of 122 laps.

Mayfield held off Jeff Gordon for the win.

"That's the way I want to win it," Mayfield said.

The other drivers all made it a point to congratulate Mayfield.

"I feel that now I'm not just a little bit accepted in this sport, but really accepted by all the drivers based on the support I've gotten from them," Mayfield said. "My answering machine was full the night after the race. I'm gonna say we had 70 or 80 calls. Not all of them left a message because it would have worn my answering machine out. I just didn't realize that I had this much support, not only in the series itself but outside the series as far as the fans and everybody involved. Probably the biggest things that have made me feel the best are the drivers, crew chiefs and car owners that have supported me. I thought most of the time when a guy wins, everybody's like, 'OK, he won.' Man, everybody that I know of that

I've seen has been just totally supportive and that's something I've been proud of most, knowing that these guys care about what I've done here."

Getting congratulated by his boyhood hero, Darrell Waltrip, is now a priceless memory of Mayfield's.

"When I was growing up, I always looked up to Darrell," Mayfield said. "I guess the first time I talked to him was on Eli Gold's show, and he was totally supportive. I was very supportive of him and I'm glad to see him running good again, just like he's glad to see me running good. I also heard from somebody that Darrell said he was handing over the torch. He told that to me. . . and that's pretty good. When you hear Darrell Waltrip saying he's handing the torch over to me, that's definitely a confidence booster and something I'm very proud of that it would come from him."

Getting the first win out of the way took off some of the pressure.

"It's a great feeling," Mayfield said. "This is the way I always felt when I was running short tracks because I was winning races. I guess it's when your confidence is up so high, it's like nothing can stop that. Nothing can slow your confidence level down. It's hard to get that when you haven't won…I'm gonna be straight up with you. I've been saying a lot, 'The win will come. I'm not worried about it.' But I have been worried about it. Not worried, just concerned that we needed to win and didn't know how to do it because we came up short so many times. It was like we just could never get the full deal going where we could pull it off, and now we know what it takes."

Ironically, the legendary Alan Kulwicki, whose unfortunate, untimely death rattled the sport, had his last win at Pocono—and Paul Andrews was his crew chief.

"For us to come back and have our first win be at Pocono in the same race, that really is pretty neat for Paul Andrews," Mayfield said. "I think we all know how close Paul and Alan were and to be able to do that says a lot. There was a lot of emotion in that win —not only Darrell Waltrip, not only our first win, but for Paul Andrews as crew chief."

NASCAR has long been a part of Mayfield's life.

"I've always been a NASCAR fan," Mayfield said. "It's something I've always wanted to do, even at a very young age."

In 1994, before coming to the Mobil Ford team, Mayfield drove for the legendary Cale Yarborough, who saw Mayfield's immense talent immediately.

"I was looking for youth and somebody I could work with," Yarborough said, "somebody I thought had talent that could be developed, and that's what I saw in Jeremy."

Liked by everyone on the Winston Cup circuit, Mayfield reciprocates that respect.

"I have several good friends that are NASCAR Winston Cup drivers, and we all try to help each other," Mayfield said. "I couldn't name a certain one that helped me more than others; there's been a lot that have helped me over my career. I know if I ever need help, there are several drivers I can go to, and I trust their judgment."

In the 1998 season opener, Mayfield was third at Daytona as Dale Earnhardt took the checkered flag.

"I can't begin to tell you how great the Daytona 500 was. The whole week was great," Mayfield said. "It was a dream week for a driver. We went down there with a really good car, and it was a really good car the whole time we were there. We tried a lot of things, but we didn't change a lot of things. Paul Andrews and the guys were on top of their game the whole time we were there. We ran the entire race without turning a screw, and we could have won the thing. It really didn't hit me until I got to the gas pumps (after the race). There were a ton of television cameras there, and they were all coming at me. Man, I looked behind me to see who they were after because I wanted to get out of their way! But they all crowded around, and we did interviews for an hour and a half. Rusty (Wallace) fought his way through them and hugged me. So did the guys on the team. It was a great, great feeling."

While Mayfield is a big fan of the Daytona track, he grew up close enough to Indiana—Owensboro is just across the river—to be a fan of the track at the Brickyard.

"It's on the same level as Daytona," Mayfield said. "It's exciting for all of us to go to Indy and try to do our best and run well there.

"When it comes to Indianapolis, I guess people would naturally think of other drivers, but the guys from Owensboro are as close to Indy as any track on the circuit," Mayfield said. "Sure, none of us grew up racing Indianapolis, but I guarantee you all of us thought about Indy when we were growing up. How could you not? Racing bicycles or, later, go-karts, everybody pretended they were winning the Daytona 500 or the Indianapolis 500. There wasn't a Brickyard 400 at the time, but if there had been, I guarantee you we would have been pretending to win that, too. I bet plenty of kids these days dream of winning the Brickyard the same way they dream of winning Daytona or the 500 at Indianapolis. There is a mystique to Indy. I think everybody feels it. Sure, you can go up there and say, 'Hey, this is just another race,' but I can't believe anybody can say that and really believe it. Man, it's Indianapolis! You can feel it long before you get in the car. There is an electricity about the place. It's the same kind of feeling you get at a Daytona or a Darlington. There is a real history to the place. You know what's gone on before you got there, and you know some pretty great things will happen long after you're gone."

Just like Mayfield's career, NASCAR continues to grow and add new tracks, something the 6-foot, 165-pound Mayfield believes to be a good thing.

"I think it's phenomenal, the growth we've all seen in the NASCAR Winston Cup Series," Mayfield said. "The expansion of the schedule is only going to add to the sport. NASCAR has done a very, very good job of promoting the sport as it is. They're just taking it to another level as far as expanding the schedule. And I'm sure they know when to not add to the schedule or make it too hard and complicated for the teams to compete."

Like many other NASCAR drivers, Mayfield does a lot of charity work. It is an effort he cherishes.

"I think, speaking for myself and hopefully other drivers, that we are very fortunate in our lives for what we get to do for a living: drive race cars," Mayfield said. "I think we should help and do things to support charities and other people who aren't as fortunate. I enjoy helping other people get what they want. I feel very fortunate for the situation that I'm in."

Mayfield's crew chief, Paul Andrews, said his driver's future is bright.

"He's shown this year (1998) and last year an amazing amount of ability and talent to take a car all the way to the end of the race—taking a bad-handling car home for a good finish," Andrews said. "That's what it takes for a good finish. Anyone can drive a good-handling car, but a good driver can take a bad-handling one in. I think he's got it."

With the higher degree of success have come higher expectations.

"I can remember early in my career when I'd be high-fiving everybody after a 15th-place finish," Mayfield said. "So the fact we can be sort of disgusted with a top-15 now says a lot."

Mayfield was never shy to ask questions of the veteran Winston Cup drivers and did just that on more than one occasion.

"The first time I raced at Darlington, I spent a lot of time asking the veteran drivers how to get around the place. What did I need to do to be successful at Darlington?" Mayfield said. "Well, I got plenty of answers, most of them really helpful. I had guys tell me the best way to shoot into the tricky first turn and how to set the car up to come out of two the best way. Other guys gave me tips on Turn 3 and how to come out of Turn 4 just right. They talked about entering the pits, which was great for me because it is a lot different here. They talked about the apron and how everyone figured that's just there for looks because it's never been used except to crash. But Darrell Waltrip probably gave me the best advice. 'Respect Darlington, and she'll respect you,' he told me. And I've never forgotten that. And I think that's helped me a great deal there. Darlington is so different than any other oval we race on. The egg shape is pretty tricky. The way you approach the first turn and the way you come off two is a whole lot different than the way you approach the third turn and the way you come off four. You set the car up to make yourself a little better at one end or the other, and then you work to make the opposite end work for you. The guys who can do that well and the guys who can really feel a race car—guys like Darrell or Earnhardt—are the ones who have been really successful there."

Those top drivers continue to impress Mayfield—even though he has now established himself as one of them.

"The best drivers seem to always have the big picture figured out," Mayfield said. "There is no doubt in my mind Mark Martin or Darrell Waltrip could, if you asked them in the middle of a race, tell you where just about every car on the racetrack was in relation to their car and which ones were in the same lap. They might not consciously go through that every lap, but they know, and you know that they know. I guess there are a couple of drivers who drive just over the nose of the car, but most are pretty savvy on what's going on and can instinctively tell you what's going to happen. So much of getting experience is developing that instinct. The more I race, and especially the more I race with guys in the Winston Cup Series, the more I think that instinct is developing for me."

Racing against the best has only made Mayfield better.

"I learn more the more laps I turn," he said. "I learn more about myself, and I learn more about the guys I'm competing against. Let's face it, there isn't a lot to learn looking at a torn up race car in the garage. There is plenty to be learned by racing with a Bill Elliott or following a Dale Earnhardt through traffic. Don't get me wrong, I want to beat Elliott and Earnhardt and Darrell and Mark and everybody else out here. But while I'm racing against them, I want to take advantage of the free education they are offering me. It's as good as a basketball player getting a University of Kentucky scholarship, and I'm sure not going to turn this 'grant-in-aid' down."

Mayfield loves hearing his idol talk about tracks.

"The way Darrell talks about Darlington is something I've paid a lot of attention to," Mayfield said. "He has reverence in his voice for the place, and it's obvious that he respects it. He almost always refers to Darlington as 'she,' and I do know there are a lot of drivers who feel the place is pretty close to human. I know this much; anybody who wins at Darlington can win anywhere. It's as true a driver's racetrack as any place I've ever raced—don't get me wrong, you still have to have a really good car."

Mayfield also enjoys racing at Bristol, which isn't far from his Kentucky roots.

"There is always a lot of electricity to the place," Mayfield said. "It's not only exciting to race at Bristol, it's exciting just to be there. When you stand in the pits and look up at those seats, man, it's almost like being in New York City. You can't help but rubberneck a little bit. Then you fill those things with close to 100,000 people— and all of them big-time race fans—and it can really be something to see. It's not hard to figure out why they are there either. Bristol has got to be one of the most exciting tracks you'll see. At least it is from a fan's perspective. It can be a pretty incredible thing to watch. Almost 40 cars crowding around a half-mile speedway running over 120 miles per hour, and every one of them trying to be the first? Man! It's pretty exciting from a driver's perspective, too. The lap times are incredible for a half-mile track. Fifteen seconds isn't much time at all. If you're not careful, a wreck can happen behind you, and you'll be back to it by the time the spotter has finished telling you about it. I've heard a lot of comparisons, but to me, Bristol is like racing inside the tub of a large automatic dryer. It throws you around, can get pretty hot, and by the end of the day, you just know somebody is going to be missing a sock or two.

"The G-forces can be incredible. There is a lot of pull going through those corners. That can really give you fits setting the chassis. It's like you head down the straightaway hard and then slam into the turns. You glide through the turns holding it as low as you can without scrubbing off a lot of speed. A lot of times, the first one back in the gas in Turns 2 or 4 is going to win the battle.

"Everything you do is crucial at Bristol. Because of the quick lap times, there isn't room for the slightest error. At other tracks, you'll do everything you can do to pick up a tenth of a second. At Bristol, you do everything you can do to pick up a thousandth of a second. That's for qualifying and the race. Every decision you make is crucial. Pitting under green at Bristol, even under the best of conditions, you are going to lose two laps. Pit at what ends up being the wrong time and you're done."

The action is fast and furious at Bristol.

"That's one of the things that makes Bristol such a cool place to run," Mayfield said. "When the blink of an eye means the difference between first and 20th, you do all you can to keep from blinking during your two qualifying laps. It's the only place I've ever seen where I had to use Murine after a qualifying run. The race is the same way. Things happen really quick at Bristol. When you are running 15-second laps, whatever happens behind you is happening in front of you pretty fast. Your spotter is crucial. Your instincts are everything. Finishing is survival; winning is survival of the fittest.

"This is a neat track," Mayfield said. "The banking is taller than some buildings in some cities, and it can be harder to get around than some of the roughest neighborhoods. If Darlington is the 'Lady in Black,' then Bristol would be the 'Mean Little Sister,' you know, the one who hides behind the couch when you're on a date as a teen-ager and yells, 'Boo!' at the worst possible times. It's like racing in a phone booth."

Mayfield has a great relationship with his teammate, Rusty Wallace.

"To have the opportunity to work with Rusty as a driver has been super," Mayfield said. "He's taken me in like a brother. He's wanting to help me, and I'm wanting to help him. All we're concerned about is the 2 car and the 12 car, nobody else."

Wallace, after initially resisting a teammate, has embraced Mayfield.

"I'll be the first to admit it, I wasn't crazy about another car in the garage," Wallace said. "But this thing was put together with a lot of business sense. We didn't go out and hire a bunch of new people and new equipment. What we're doing is pooling resources."

That pooling has increased the reservoir of confidence Mayfield possesses.

"It's brought my confidence up," Mayfield said. "The whole deal in general has my confidence at the highest level."

Mayfield's crew chief, Paul Andrews, agrees.

"Everything is an open book on both sides," Andrews said. "We share information 100 percent; there's nothing we hide from Rusty or vice versa. There are no secrets. We have meetings on Monday mornings after a race, and everybody is involved, key personnel. We talk about the race and what each other did. Even during the race, we're talking to each other. The goal is to make both cars as good as they possibly can be, and hopefully we'll end up with two really good cars."

Mayfield made his Winston Cup debut in October 1993 at Charlotte Speedway. Driving for Sadler Brothers—a team Mayfield had joined three years earlier as a fabricator—Mayfield qualified 30th and finished 29th.

The Winston Cup success is an old dream of Mayfield's.

"It was always a dream—that's what's funny, it's become a reality thing now," Mayfield said. "It was a dream at one time, and it's turned into something that's more than a dream. I'd always wanted all of this to happen, so my career has gone pretty good. I got a little bit thrown at me instead of a bunch thrown on me at one time. I got to experience everything a little bit at a time and that's probably helped me more than anything. When I started, nothing was going for me; then all of a sudden, the little pieces started coming together better and better. That's the way I've looked at my whole deal."

The hard work has paid off—and just the mere fact that Mayfield has paid his dues along the way is something he treasures.

"I wouldn't trade the way my career has gone for anything because it's made me respect everything more," Mayfield said. "Nothing's ever been given to me. It's just rolled into place, and it's going to help more in the long run.

"I started racing when I was 13 years old, and that's all I wanted to do—to win. If I was racing go-karts, I wanted to win every go-kart race I could get into. When I set my sights a little higher, I did whatever I had to do to get where I wanted to go. I worked as a fabricator for Earl Sadler to get my first Winston Cup ride, and I did a lot of the fabricating work when I drove for Cale Yarborough. That's what it took to get me where I wanted to go. Now I'm here. I'm where I've always wanted to be, with a top-notch team that is going places. This is a dream come true for me. I worked hard to get here, and I appreciate what I have."

To be a consistent winner on the Winston Cup circuit, Mayfield says you must first be a consistent contender.

"To finish in the top five consistently you have to learn to run in the top 10," Mayfield said. "To win races you have to learn to run in the top five. We've been consistent, and we've been a good consistent. That's what it takes to win in this sport. To be a solid contender week in and week out is the key to not only winning races but to being strong in the points."

For Mayfield, the passion to race runs deep. And he feels that passion before every race.

"Every race is important and every race is pretty exciting," Mayfield said. "There is no comparison to hearing 'Gentlemen, start your engines,' and hearing your engine and 41 others roar to life. And that's the case no matter where it is or what kind of racing it is. I get the same butterflies now that I got when I cranked my Late Model stock."

Mayfield has also improved on road courses, something he didn't get a lot of experience doing as he raced on short track ovals growing up.

"I didn't grow up on road courses," Mayfield said. "When I was a kid, I didn't lay there and dream of zipping through the esses and blasting through the chicane. I mean, my dreams were steep banks and blasting down backstretches. But I like road courses and I like running them. It's like some of those video games. You always start with the oval stuff because it's what you're used to, but you usually head to the road courses sooner or later. It's a challenge. It's fun.

How many opportunities do you get to take a 3,400-pound piece of metal and throw it through a turn? Well, I guess we'll get 90 opportunities through the horseshoe at Watkins Glen, but it's a real challenge for a driver."

The road courses are just another challenge—and an essential one at that.

"That's one of the things that makes the Winston Cup and running for the points so special," Mayfield said. "If you're going to be like Earnhardt or Petty—and win championships—you can't specialize. You have to be good everywhere. They pay the same amount of points at Watkins Glen as they do at Daytona or Indy or anywhere else. Lose your focus on that at any track, and you're going to be in a lot of trouble really quickly."

While a lot has changed, Mayfield—as a person—has not. He is still grounded and eager to meet new people and go to new places.

"I've changed in confidence only," Mayfield said. "I think I'm still Jeremy. I don't think you'll ever change that. I'm not going to be any different, but I think my confidence level is definitely sky-high when I get in that race car, not anywhere else, but just when I get in that car I feel really good about it. I've got a lot of confidence in my equipment and my team, and when you've got that, that's all you need."

Andrews agrees.

"In Jeremy I haven't really seen any change," Andrews said. "His confidence is way up. It doesn't matter what kind of sport you're in or what kind of business you run, if your confidence is up, you're going to do better, and his confidence is way up right now."

The mix of young and veteran talent can do nothing but help NASCAR continue to grow.

"I think it's great for the sport," Mayfield said. "You've not only got the veteran drivers running good, now you've got some younger guys like Jeff Gordon, Jeff Burton, myself and Bobby Labonte. It's a mix and I think the sport needs that. It certainly doesn't hurt anything. We've got a good combination of drivers, and it's a mix that brings a lot of different fan types into the sport. I think it covers just about everyone it can cover."

CHAPTER 16

MIKE MCLAUGHLIN

McLaughlin memo: Finished third in the 1998 Busch Grand National points standings; won at New Hampshire driving a NASCAR Busch Series Grand National Division car in 1990, then capped the day by winning the NASCAR Modified race as well; has at least one victory in each of three different NASCAR divisions; won NASCAR Modified Tour's Most Popular Driver award in 1985; won NASCAR Modified Tour championship in 1988; won Most Popular Driver award in NASCAR Busch North Series in 1992 and 1993; finished third in 1993 NASCAR Busch North Series; won "homecoming" race at Watkins Glen International in 1997; posted first two-win season in NASCAR Busch Series career in 1997; named NASCAR Busch Series Grand National Division Most Popular Driver for 1997; won Bud Pole for 1998 NASCAR Busch Series race at Daytona.

"Magic Shoes" knows when to hit the gas. Mike McLaughlin has emerged as one of the stars of the Busch Grand National Series. He joined the Frank Cicci/Scott Welliver-owned team in 1994 when Todd Bodine moved to the Winston Cup series. The following year, McLaughlin was third in the final Busch Grand National points standings. His first win came at Dover in 1995.

"It is tough to get the right opportunity," said McLaughlin, who was born on Oct. 6, 1956, and counts snowmobiling, riding his Harley-Davidson, water-skiing and working out among his hobbies. "I was very fortunate that Frank Cicci, Scott and Jeff Welliver and John Gitler, the team owners, had the confidence in me. You need to be around long enough to show some results. And a lot of people with ability have never been given the right chance. I have."

When Bodine rejoined the team in 1997, both drivers excelled with Bodine taking second in the points standings and McLaughlin claiming fourth place—and he was named the Most Popular Driver for the BGN series that year.

Being on a team helps drivers. "It's an advantage because the information is wide open. If you need anything, comparing notes, one car is going better than the other, you can use their setup," McLaughlin said.

McLaughlin competed for seven years in the NASCAR Modifieds, winning the championship in 1988. One of his biggest days came in 1990 when he won the doubleheader—the Modified and Busch North races in a single day at New Hampshire International. Along with a victory at Watkins Glen, the New Hampshire double-win was a big moment.

"It was awesome, overwhelming," McLaughlin said. "That day in 1990 is the highlight of my career. I won the Busch North race and celebrated in Victory Lane. Five minutes later, I had to refocus and get into a Modified car. At the end of that race, I ended up back in Victory Lane for the second time that day. It was unbelievable. It was wild because you got one car, didn't even get to enjoy it. Then you're swapping suits and getting into another car, getting on the line and getting ready to roll. And to be back in Victory Lane again was awesome. Watkins Glen was pretty big. I have a lot of friends in that area. It's pretty tough to say which one was bigger. It was wild at Watkins Glen."

Winning on the road course at Watkins Glen was also important because there were so many Winston Cup regulars competing.

"I enjoy racing against the Cup guys; it makes it more rewarding when you beat them—I think it's good because it makes the Busch regulars work harder. Most of the time they beat us, but it does make it more rewarding when you do put one by them, like at Watkins Glen. That was just an awesome race; we had something going from Tuesday on, functions and other events."

McLaughlin came away with a third-place in the 1993 Busch North points race.

"I think the North Series is a great series," McLaughlin said. "There are a lot of good drivers there. I know there is a lot of talent and there will be a lot more to follow."

McLaughlin is more than "just" a driver, taking great pride in his outstanding shop abilities as a fabricator and car builder.

"I spend a lot of time in the shop doing some fabricating when needed, sheet metal. And working with setups. But I've got a great group of guys to where I don't have to worry about anything. They cover all the bases, so I have all the confidence in the world when I jump in that car. I was fortunate, my dad had a fabricating shop. He was a blacksmith. He had a lot of tools that I used to fabricate with. And I built my first car to run on a local dirt track, and it just continued from there."

His nickname follows him everywhere.

"That was given to me by a guy named Joe Morada, a track announcer," McLaughlin said. "A lot of guys had the name 'Hot Shoes,' other stuff like that. Barefoot Bob McReady, and Jumpin' Jack Johnson, AJ Slideways, Alan Johnson, all those guys had nicknames and I ended up with one, too. He called me Magic Shoes. It stuck, that's for sure. Back when I was racing in the Dirt Modified . . . I won a race in the last lap, back then everybody was considered a 'Hotshoe.' By doing that, the announcer came up with 'Magic Shoes.' And it's followed me for five series."

A ride in the Winston Cup series might be down the line, but McLaughlin focuses only on the task at hand.

"Right now," he said, "I am just trying to be more successful where I am. I want to win races and be more consistent. I definitely would like to win a Busch Grand National championship as soon as I can. Winning the championship and winning the most races, that would be a successful season. I've had one year like that, the year I won the Modified title. They are few and far between, but you just have to keep digging."

McLaughlin traces his racing roots back to his hometown in New York.

"I was raised in Waterloo, a town with a little dirt track, so that's probably where I got the bug. I have several people I looked up to. At the age of 20 I decided to build my own race car—a dirt modified—and it has taken off from there. Back then you could build your own car and be relatively successful. It's a lot harder today."

While he's had a lot of success on the road courses, McLaughlin still enjoys the longer tracks.

"I always look forward to the big tracks—Daytona and Talladega are wild," he said. "I haven't had the results there, though. But to me, every racetrack is a challenge; I guess the best racetracks are the ones with more than one groove, where you can do a lot of side-by-side racing, whether it's short track, intermediate or super-speedway. I like Talladega. It's probably the most fun. Wide open all day, bumper to bumper and side by side. What better racing is there than that?"

With so many new tracks for the NASCAR Winston Cup, Busch Grand National and Craftsman Truck series, the drivers have to constantly be ready for new challenges, and that's something McLaughlin enjoys.

"I enjoy going to new tracks," McLaughlin said. "It makes the whole experience new and exciting."

CHAPTER 17

JERRY NADEAU

Nadeau's adieu: Finished rookie season on Winston Cup series 36th in the points standings; qualified ninth in the Jiffy Lube 300 at New Hampshire International Speedway in 1997; won silver medal at Nations Cup VII co-driving at Donington Park, England, in 1997; in 1993 he earned two poles and a win on the Barber Pro Series and five top-four finishes on the IMSA Firestone Firehawk Series; won the 1991 Barber Pro Series title, a year after winning the series' Rookie of the Year Award.

Although he is only in his twenties, Jerry Nadeau has plenty of driving time behind him—he started at age four. At age seven, Nadeau somehow steered around rules and started winning trophies in the 8-12-year-old division at a track in Bethany, near his New England hometown of Danbury, Connecticut.

A lot of Nadeau's inspiration and guidance came from his father.

"My dad is the greatest," Nadeau said. "He got me started racing when I was four. I used to race at Danbury Racearena, which was only a mile from home. He was big influence; he got me where I am. I left home at an early age, at 18, but he really pushed me. He got me to run hard no matter what kind of equipment I had. He's been great. He comes to the races when he can get away from work. And hopefully when he gets closer to retirement, he can come spend more time with me. I'd really enjoy that."

From 1984 when he was 14, to 1990, Nadeau won 10 kart championships. In 1991 his career made a big move. That was when he ran 12 races in the Skip Barber 8-Day Speedweek. Nadeau, who first ran the series three years earlier in 1991, won eight races and took rookie of the year honors. The following year he won the series championship. From there, he added the 12 Hours of Sebring endurance race, the IMSA Firestone Firehawk Series, and a different form of racing in the form of the 1993 European Formula Ford Festival. Two years later, in 1995, Nadeau got his first opportunity behind the wheel of a NASCAR stock car, driving test sessions in a NASCAR Busch Series Grand National Division machine.

Nadeau returned to the Formula Open European Union Series in 1996, although the previous year he had moved to Charlotte, North Carolina, to work on his budding NASCAR career.

"We had a lot of fun," Nadeau says of his Formula Open stint. "And I feel like the competition is just as fierce there as it is here. I was pretty excited about doing that deal."

In 1997, Nadeau took over the No. 1 Pontiac on the Winston Cup Series after Morgan Shepherd moved on to a different ride. But that was short-lived because sponsorship concerns forced Nadeau to leave that ride. The 1998 season brought plenty of promise, as Bill Elliott was expanding his team to a two-car format for 1998, in a co-op effort with FIRSTPLUS and its public pitch man, Miami Dolphin quarterback Dan Marino, in a Ford. The car had the familiar Miami paint scheme of green, white and orange, and also sported Marino's famous No. 13. Nadeau was released but has rebounded in outstanding fashion. Nadeau didn't miss a beat and stayed close to Kenny Irwin Jr. in the rookie points race by hopping directly into the Cartoon Network Melling Racing Ford.

"We think Jerry is a talented young driver who would be an asset for any team," said Melling Racing Enterprises vice president Mark Melling. "Given the fact that he has seen most of the tracks already this year, he should have a strong second half of the season."

The change in teams might have temporarily stalled any driver, but not Nadeau.

"Actually, it's been pretty easy for me, considering the circumstances," Nadeau said. "I started with Elliott-Marino Motorsports, which was a brand new team. Situations happen, and I was let go. But Mark Melling called and gave me the chance to drive for the whole year. The biggest difference is the team has been around, the cars and engines are competitive. It makes it easier for me, I can concentrate on racing. It just takes some time, and I'm in it for the long haul."

Ironically, there is no bad blood between Nadeau and the popular Elliott.

"I have nothing against Bill and those guys," Nadeau said. "As a matter of fact, I still go over there and talk. I had a real good relationship with those guys on the team. It's just chemistry. To be honest, in this new deal with the Mellings, it just feels like I melted right into this deal, with Lake Speed resigning and me not missing a race. It is easier. I've got a great veteran crew chief, Jeff Buice, and the Cartoon Network people are great. And FIRSTPLUS is still an associate sponsor on this car, and they're great. We're just taking it slow and running hard and hoping that something comes together for next year."

Despite the switch in teams, Nadeau's qualifying efforts showed no signs of decline.

"It's not easy for a rookie to jump in with two teams and try to make races. The biggest thing for rookies is to make the race," Nadeau said. "You get 48-50 cars at a race that are competitive. And being new guys, we still have to be competitive right off the bat. I feel like we're learning a lot."

More than ever before, Nadeau is getting the hang of racing on ovals.

"I feel like we'll get our first win on a road course, but we like a lot of ovals," Nadeau said. "I feel like I'm lacking the ability to be able to tell the crew what I need. I feel like right now I'm only at 50 percent. I've got a lot to learn. I know I can win some of these races. It's just a matter of time. I know we'll have a good run here soon."

Perhaps the reason for Nadeau's optimism for future success at road courses is that he did well at both Sears Point and Watkins Glen—both road courses—during the 1998 season.

"Sears Point was pretty exciting because we qualified on the outside of the pole," Nadeau said. "But then we broke a piece and crashed out. At Watkins Glen we qualified eighth and ran well all day, then finished 15th. A lot of races have been fun—just to be in Winston Cup is great. I'm smiling every day, and hopefully we'll be up front soon."

While it might seem to many that Nadeau jumped feet-first into Winston Cup—bypassing what has become the traditional few years on the Busch circuit—Nadeau claims he is pleased with his timing.

"The series has changed over the last three years, dramatically," Nadeau said. "I feel like it's the best time to get into Winston Cup racing. I felt like I was going to make it because I had the desire, whether it was CART, Formula One or NASCAR. The way they run the sport is great. Like they say, 'it's the fastest growing sport in America.' It's a fun sport. We're racing almost every weekend. We barely have enough time to get home and wash our clothes before we have to leave again. But that's why I'm here, and I plan to be doing it for a long time."

Driving in the Winston Cup Series has also provided Nadeau with access to the top drivers in the world. The effect of that association and interaction can't go unnoticed.

"I talk to a lot of guys in the pits," Nadeau said. "The ones that I really go after are the two best in Winston Cup, Mark Martin and Jeff Gordon. The neat thing is they're both my size, so I can look eye-to-eye with them. They won't steer you wrong. They're there for help. Not many people go to them for help, but for guys that are new, rookies, they're the best. And John Andretti too, he goes to all the rookie meetings."

The domination by those two—Martin and Gordon—and the lack of others as legitimate shots at the points championship, with the exception of a few others, including Jeff Burton, Dale Jarrett, the Labonte brothers and Rusty Wallace, is something everyone notices, but few can do anything about.

"Some of these teams that have been around have gotten better," Nadeau said. "And some of these others just haven't stepped up. I don't think NASCAR likes it, itself. The same guys winning week in and week out doesn't sell as many tickets. I think they'd like to see a variety of drivers. If you're a true race fan, you don't care if the same guys win. I remember Harry Gant won four in a row, and nobody thought that was boring. Some guys lead all day, and others lead at the end. I think the guys that are winning all the time are just meant to win."

One of those at the rookie meetings is Kenny Irwin Jr., who Nadeau says was set up perfectly to win Rookie of the Year.

"I don't think our team is the caliber of the Yates team," Nadeau said. "And Kenny (Irwin) has really been tutored well by Dale Jarrett. Those guys were built to win the rookie award."

Nadeau's rookie year introduction included a wreck at Talladega. "Everything was going good until about halfway through the race," Nadeau said. "We were about fourth or fifth in line on the outside. The first thing I saw was a little smoke, so I lifted. Next, I was seeing a windshield flying by and hitting me in my windshield. Then I had oil on my windshield and couldn't see anything at all. So the first thing I had to do was look right and see how close I was to the wall. I kind of followed the rail of the wall to see where I was going. The first car I hit was Dale Earnhardt; I actually put him back on his wheels. Then I was hard in the brakes. That's when Chad Little came across the track and I got into him."

Nadeau tried to avoid Little, but couldn't.

"A driver can't do everything," Nadeau said. "I mean, he's going so fast, and the cars can only stop so fast. You've just got to hope luck is on your side and God pulls you through. The biggest thing is that everyone is OK after a big wreck like that. I know some people love to look at that saying, 'Oh, wow, look at the big wreck.' But it's not a good thing for us. I mean, we work our butts off on those cars. You know, we worked about three months on that car."

While success at the Winston Cup level didn't come immediately, don't expect to see Nadeau change gears and leave NASCAR for open-wheel division racing.

"My plan is to be in Winston Cup racing until it's no longer there," he said. "I've worked my butt off to get this far, and I don't plan on getting out and moving on like a lot of other people have done."

And Nadeau still has plenty of folks believing in him.

"Jerry Nadeau is a very gifted race driver with an immense amount of untapped raw talent," said ESPN television commentator Derek Daly, whose driving experience includes Formula One and CART Indy cars. "I believe in the very near future that his name will be recognized universally throughout motorsports."

CHAPTER 18

STEVE PARK

Park's place: Finished second in NASCAR Featherlite Modified Tour championship in 1995 and '96; won three races, finished third in points, and was named Raybestos Rookie of the Year in NASCAR Busch Series Grand National Division in 1997.

If progress is sometimes one step forward and two steps back, then Steve Park is due for several quantum leaps forward after a rough Winston Cup rookie season in 1998.

Yet, if the past is an indication of the future, Park's best days will be far more memorable than what turned out to be a forgettable rookie season on the Winston Cup Series in 1998. Park had 22 poles and 15 wins while on the NASCAR Featherlite Modified Tour where he was named the Most Popular Driver in 1995. (Park's father, Bob, is a long-time Modified driver.) Park won his first Modified race in 1988 and followed that with five wins in 1989— on his own team.

While Park made his mark with his driving skills, he credits the racing entrepreneurs who helped put the Northeast on NASCAR's map.

"I think one of the biggest things to really get drivers noticed in the Northeast was the inception of the New Hampshire International Speedway that Bob and Gary Bahre built," Park said. "They gave us an opportunity to showcase our talents in front of some of the guys from the NASCAR Winston Cup and NASCAR Busch Series. So, I would say it was really the inception of the New Hampshire International Speedway up in New Hampshire."

Park then moved on to the NASCAR Busch Series, buying a third-hand car and trying an unsuccessful, unsponsored stint.

A blown engine at New Hampshire signaled the end of the NASCAR Busch Series excursion and pushed Park to the financial brink.

"I was just flat out of money," Park said. "That was definitely the low point of my career. I was out of money, and I didn't even have my Modified racing to turn to because I sold all the equipment."

Park returned to the track to work with his father's car. A break came when Modified owner Curt Chase saw Park working in the pits and Chase asked Park to drive his car. Park spent 1991 and 1992 with Chase, moving on to TG racing where he picked up 14 wins in just two years. In 1995, Park notched seven wins with Sheba Racing and followed with another five victories in 1996. That year, Park started fewer than a dozen races in the NASCAR Busch North Series, yet drove to wins at Nazareth and New Hampshire.

"Running the Late Model division, open-wheel and full body has helped me," Park said. "I think probably the majority of help I had was running the Busch Series up north; it simulates the weight of the cars down here. Plus the driving skills you learn in the Modified Division, to go along with that, has probably been the biggest help."

When he first left the North Series for the Busch Grand National, Park hoped his fans didn't feel like he was abandoning them. Just the opposite proved to be the case.

"The fans have been great," Park said. "I really thought when I left New England that I might be leaving my fans behind, not that I wanted to, but it might have happened. But I found out that I had more fans than I ever knew. The support I've received down here from the New England area has been great. That's been important to know that I have all those fans behind me even though I've taken a new path. I want to spend as much time making myself available to meet with as many fans as I can. And, of course, we want to put on a great race for them. I just can't tell you how excited I am about going back up there and having this opportunity."

Park made a big impression at Watkins Glen in 1996 when Joe Nemechek asked Park to qualify Nemechek's truck in the NASCAR Craftsman Truck Series. Nemechek told Park to "just get the car in the field."

Park did better than just qualify Nemechek's truck—Park grabbed the pole and grabbed plenty of attention for the performance.

"That was the third time I'd ever been to Watkins Glen and the first time I'd ever been in a truck," Park said. "I've run a Busch North race there and a Modified race.

"I think probably one of my biggest strengths, something other people have pointed out, is my adaptability at tracks I haven't been in before," Park said. "So I'd have to say it is my adaptability for different tracks and different cars."

Racing at Watkins Glen provides another challenge for drivers because it is a road course as opposed to the ovals. Park has honed his road course skills by training at three different road racing schools.

"Bill Cooper at Bob Bondurant's road racing school told me if I stayed on the course and didn't break my race car I'd finish in the top 10," Park said the week of a race at Watkins Glen. "I think that sums it up. If you can drive conservative enough not to run off the course and not manhandle the car too much to a point where you break it, run all the laps and be there at the end, you're going to finish in the top 10 or top five and have a chance to win the race. Some guys go there with the thought that they don't really like road racing. I think a lot of the oval track guys have adapted well to road racing the last three or four years. With the different driving schools out there, you can get some pretty good lessons in road racing. I think it's helping me not only to be a better road racer but also a better oval track racer."

Park, born on Aug. 23, 1963, was the driver of the No. 3 Chevrolet owned by Dale and Teresa Earnhardt in 1997 in the Busch Grand National Division.

Earnhardt actually tried to contact Park sooner. But Park thought the message left on his answering machine by a voice claiming to be the Intimidator was just some friends playing a joke. It actually was Earnhardt, who left a second message, stating that he had already left one (unreturned) message.

"I grew up watching and looking up to Dale Earnhardt," Park said. "I must admit, he was a bit intimidating to me at first. He's not intimidating anymore. He's a great teacher to have, and he's kind of taken me under his wing."

The native of East Northport, New York, had the best-ever debut by a Busch Grand National rookie, winning three races, 20 finishes in the top 10 and almost $700,000 in prize money. For those efforts, Park was a clear choice as the winner of the Raybestos Rookie of the Year honor.

As a Busch Series rookie at Talladega, Park was trying to pass Mark Martin before settling for second place behind the talented Martin. However, Park did get a boost from Dale Earnhardt Sr., who was helping from the pits.

"Earnhardt was giving me guidance on a slingshot pass and how to execute it, how to use the car behind me as an advantage to get by Mark," Park said. "Generally, the role he plays on the team is pretty hands-on. But he pays us to do our jobs, and he lets us do our jobs. He doesn't give us specific orders from his pit area. Tony Eury does a great job with the car. Dale just sits back and watches, and if he feels that his experience can lend something, then he lets us know. It's more of a guidance thing.

"I was giving it all I had there at the end. He was just using up a lot of racetrack. We tried everything in the book to get by Mark, but he was just a little bit too strong," Park said. "We tried the high line and the low line. We even tried to go through the infield. He was just too strong. Dale was helping me, and when you've got him on your side, especially when you're drafting, you can't go wrong. We gave 'em everything we had. Mark had a strong car, and he was driving his heart out. I was driving my heart out. We just came up second."

That race at Talladega was frustrating to Park because he didn't have a lot of laps at a superspeedway under his belt, something all drivers need to make the most of their ride. Still, that race was Park's third straight top-10 finish in April of the 1997 Busch Grand National season.

"I'd have to say the lack of experience probably did hurt, to be perfectly honest," Park said. "That was only my second super-speedway race, and it probably takes years to learn the mastery of the draft...everywhere I go I learn a lot in a short time. It will be a while before I'm real comfortable on a superspeedway. To finish second to Mark Martin in a Busch race, that's still a big accomplishment."

The bulk of Earnhardt's advice actually came before the race.

"Right before we came to Talladega the first time, Dale took me in his office and drew the track out on a napkin," Park said. "He showed me the best line to take to get around the place, and he even pointed out the bumps on the track. When I got out there on the track, sure enough, those bumps were right where he said they would be."

Going from the open-wheel Modifieds to the Busch and Winston Cup cars was quite a change for Park.

"It was difficult to move from the Modified to the Busch Series," Park said. "The main reason is the weight; that's been the biggest change. The Busch car is a lot heavier, and it also runs on a lot narrower tire, and it's a radial tire—the weight of the cars, the size of the cars, and the fact that you can't see where the front tires are.

I would say those factors, the transition period, and of course, the new racetracks are the biggest adjustments."

After impressing the Earnhardts, Park moved up to Winston Cup for the 1998 season driving the No. 1 Pennzoil Chevy.

That Park was able to make the Winston Cup—and work for Earnhardt—should tell others to set their sights high.

"I also consider myself to be very fortunate to not only be associated with NASCAR, but also with Dale Earnhardt Inc. I think it's motivational to know that a pretty much middle-class guy from New England can do this and come down South and work for Dale Earnhardt," Park said. "It should be a motivating thing for everyone that if you work hard and go after it, you can realize it."

Park is fortunate that the Pennzoil Chevy owner is a NASCAR legend, and Park has learned a lot from Earnhardt.

"By race day, Dale and I have probably spent a lot of time over the weekend talking, not only about racing but setups for the cars, everything that comes into getting ready for Sunday," Park said. "Come race day morning, usually we are pretty focused on our own, on the job at hand, and that's winning. So usually there is more communication during the week than there is on Sunday morning."

Park's competitive streak runs deep. "I don't like to lose, no matter what I'm doing," Park said. "Sometimes that's good and sometimes that's bad. I'm not that good in a supermarket with a shopping cart because I always try to cut people off."

Sounds just like his boss.

"Dale's a smart race car driver," Park said. "He thrives on being smart. You have to be aggressive at times, but you have to finish the race in order to win the race. Being stupid and running flat out at times when you're not supposed to is not the right way to go about it. I've got a lot to learn—but I've got the best teacher in the world. Failure is not an option. I'm going to work hard and do what I have to do to be successful—not only for Dale Earnhardt, but for myself."

So while his boss is the "Intimidator," Park is far from intimidated.

"He puts his pants on one leg at a time, just like you and I do,"

Park said. "And just like you and I do, he has his up days and his down days. But most of the time, he's in a pretty good mood. He's been really good to me, real patient. He gave me a great opportunity at the beginning of the year, and he's been real supportive. He's been extremely helpful giving me some insight on the tracks I've never run before. If there's ever a question in my mind that I need to get answered, I can just pick up the phone and call him. He's just awesome."

The Intimidator returns the respect.

"He's got a lot to learn," Earnhardt said, "but I think he'll be a quick learner."

Teresa Earnhardt saying that Park made a big impression on the Intimidator speaks for itself.

"Steve Park impressed Dale Earnhardt," she said, "and it's not easy to impress Dale Earnhardt."

Park looked like he was in a position to compete with Kenny Irwin Jr. and Jerry Nadeau for the Raybestos Rookie of the Year Award on the Winston Cup Series in 1998 until Park was involved in a horrible crash during practice at Atlanta in March. Park suffered a fractured right femur, broken left collarbone, broken right shoulder blade and two broken teeth.

The crash—an investigation pointed out—was caused by a flat tire.

"We had everything analyzed on the front of the car," Park said. "But it's kind of like trying to decide which came first, the chicken or the egg, there was so much damage. But through our analysis, we determined that we had a suspension failure on the right front side which caused the shock absorber to puncture the right front tire, which inevitably caused the wreck."

Park's memory of the crash itself is somewhat blurry.

"I only remember the car was running great, and we were all pumped up," he said. "We were doing qualifying runs just trying to make sure the car was fast enough for a top-five or to sit on the front row. It was just a routine day. Something happened in Turn 4. I think something broke on the right front of the Pennzoil car and made it do a hard right into the retaining wall. That is all I remember until I woke up with the workers pulling me out of the car."

Part of Park's rehabilitation was mental—he felt like he needed to drive to complete the healing process.

"I am feeling great. I think I will be 100 percent when I get the opportunity to race again at the Brickyard," Park said at the time. "But all kidding aside, the leg is about 95 percent healed. Mentally I will be back to 100 percent when I get back to doing what I love to do, and that's racing."

Accidents are just a part of auto racing, something all drivers must endure at one time or another.

"This is something that is part of the sport," Park said. "I hate that it came during my rookie season. I wanted a good clean season to get some track time. I've had a lot of support from the drivers who've been through this before. Kyle Petty's been by and so has Bill Elliott. Those guys have been through this and have been real encouraging."

Petty had a leg break similar to Park's.

"Kyle has been very supportive," Park said. "He has made me laugh through this whole ordeal. He helped me through this crisis, but told me he expected me to help someone else through a crisis down the road."

Darrell Waltrip, struggling as a driver/owner, replaced Park and fared very well, something the Earnhardts—and Park himself—appreciated.

"I feel that D.W. has done a great job really taking this team to the next level, from being a startup team to one that has grown to being capable of winning a race before the year is out," Park said. "So we have been real proud of his accomplishments in the car as a driver, and what he has been able to accomplish helping the team grow."

Park did return in time during the 1998 season to run at the Brickyard.

"The Brickyard, to me, is something similar to the Daytona

500," Park said. "To have the opportunity to run the Brickyard is realizing a dream I had as a small boy, which was to compete at Indianapolis. Previously it would have only been in the Indy 500, but now that NASCAR has made its way to Indianapolis, I get to compete at the Brickyard."

Since Park jumped from the Busch Grand National to Winston Cup after only really one full season on the Busch Series, he was able to give some direction to Dale Earnhardt Jr., who dominated the Busch Series in 1998.

"We have gotten close the last couple of years," Park said. "He's a great race car driver, and he has a great future here at DEI. Being a rookie on the NASCAR Busch Series, he has leaned on me a little bit as far as my experience with the series and the team a year ago. I enjoy working with him, and I know there's great things ahead for us both at Dale Earnhardt Inc."

While out, Park made his debut as a broadcaster, giving him a different vantage point to watch the races.

"For the broadcasting debut, one thing that I learned is that there are a lot of similarities between broadcasting and racing," Park said. "Really, it's a team effort. In the broadcast booth, to do a good job, there is a lot more that goes into it than you actually see on TV. I was amazed that there are so many similarities between racing as a team sport and broadcasting."

Park did drive—sort of—while he was injured, playing the NASCAR Racing 2 video game.

"When I first got hurt, the people from Papyrus who manufacture the games sent me a steering wheel with the gas pedal and a brake pedal on the steering wheel, so I could still play," Park said. "Without a doubt I think it helps; from a timing standpoint, it can help keep you sharp on the racetrack."

Before the 1998 season began, Park had started a training program. He credits that commitment to fitness with speeding his return from the crash.

"Before the accident I started a routine—which I wouldn't say was religious—but learning the effects of working out before the injury, and how it made my recovery faster," Park said. "I have taken up working out pretty religiously since the accident, right up until today. . . I have been at it three days a week, pretty hard. I feel like I am in the best shape of my life."

So Park has chalked the whole year up to learning.

"I would like to say that it has been a year that we have grown as a team," Park said. "We have learned from it and put the adversity behind us so we can look to the future and look toward winning some races."

Another factor to Park's success is that he knows how the cars are set up and what causes certain things to happen to the car, and he shares that freely with his crew chief.

"It's something I have developed over years of racing," Park said. "It's important that you communicate what is going on in the car to your crew chief so you can cure some problems during a race or in setup. I don't really listen to other drivers, so I don't know what they do, but we really feel that the communication I have with the crew chief is something that is really going to help us develop a winning way on the racetrack."

While "time off" are two words not often uttered during the season—or in the off-season, for that matter—Park does try to keep his other interests alive to maintain his focus and perspective.

"We run from Pocono and the Brickyard straight out to the end of the year, so we won't have any weekends off," Park said. "But we try to give me and the guys on the team one day off a week. That's when you try and make up for the rest of the schedule that we're on. What I like to do is a little boating, or what I mentioned before, riding my motorcycle. That's what I like to do when I'm not racing."

A NASCAR veteran despite his young age, Park is also a lifelong NASCAR fan.

"I've been racing in NASCAR since I was 16. I've been a big fan of NASCAR racing," Park said. "A person I looked up to was my dad, and not because I drive for him. Like a lot of people, I've always been a big Dale Earnhardt fan. Seven Winston Cup titles, a great driving style, and a unique personality—that's what made me a Dale Earnhardt fan. Over the last four or five years, Jeff Gordon too. He's been able to accomplish something that I have been wanting to accomplish, and he's done it at roughly the same age, so that's pretty neat."

As for advice to young drivers, Park keeps it simple and to the point. "I think just be successful at no matter what you are doing—Street Stock, Modified, Busch North, whatever," Park said. "Strive hard to be the best you can, and try to promote yourself and the sport the best you can. Research what you want to do, and be sure because it takes a 110 percent commitment. It's a challenge, but it's very rewarding. It's been awesome."

While 1998 wasn't everything Park had hoped for on the track, he was able to do something that he had always dreamed of—helping his father rejoin Modified racing as a driver. "The tables are turned a bit," Park said. "He gave me my first start in a car, so I guess it's only fair."

The 6-foot, 175-pound Park, an avid golfer, lists his father as his hero. So when Bob Park, at age 55, went back to driving a car for the Southern Modified Auto Racing teams, Park was there—physically, emotionally and financially.

"Your mom and dad do so much for you from the day you are born that anything you can do later in life to make their lives more enjoyable is certainly worth it," Park said. "My dad's biggest love in his life, besides his family, is racing. He had the time and I had the money to help him so we decided to go racing again. I was pretty excited and told him I'd help him as much as I could. It's kind of fun to see him thinking about driving again just like he was when I was growing up."

Bob Park is no stranger to racing, having competed in the NASCAR Featherlite Modified Series as well as some ARCA, Busch North and Busch South races. But with a full-time job as a gear specialist for a trucking firm, Bob only had evenings to put into racing, when he would work on cars in his garage.

"Racing has always been in my blood," Bob said. "I never made a lot of money at it, but it gave me some very good times with good friends and family and that is worth more than money to me."

Bob is no novice on the track—he finished second in Modified tour season standings in the early '80s.

"Just the other day I was reading a racing newspaper and they wrote something about a race I won at Riverhead and that brought back a lot of pleasant memories," said Bob Park. "I don't have any dreams of making this a career again, but it would be nice to do well. This will be more like a hobby."

Bob and his wife, Dotti, ended up moving from New York to North Carolina to be closer to Steve for the 1998 season. In addition, Bob was hired by Dale Earnhardt Inc., as a gear specialist. Dotti runs Steve's fan club from North Carolina.

The heat will be up even higher on Steve Park next year to prove two things: First, that his quick success in the Busch Series wasn't a fluke, and secondly, that he truly belongs on the Winston Cup division.

"You learn," Park said, "to live with some pressure in this business."

One person firmly behind Park is Earnhardt. "This kid is good, or we wouldn't have him where he is today," Earnhardt said. "He's a quick learner and has patience for someone with his limited experience in these big cars. He's got a lot of learning to do, but he wants to win, and that's why he's with us."

Park has others who see a long, bright future for him. "Steve Park is tomorrow's race driver today," said Chris Economaki, National Speed Sport news editor. "He's skilled at the wheel, polished in his mien and, when the sun goes down, sartorially elegant."

"He's good, and he's got the right kind of mental attitude to deal with this sport," said veteran crew chief Philippe Lopez. "Steve is a quick learner."

The challenges are there, and so is Park. "It's not been easy," Park said. "But it's pretty incredible how my life and driving career have turned out in the last few years. I can't wait to see what happens in the next few years."

While the 1998 season was trying at times, it did provide Park with a lifelong memory: While Park was making his debut in the Daytona 500, Earnhardt, who had more than 20 starts in the race, won his first-ever Daytona 500.

"Both Dale and I realized our dreams," said Park, who started 33rd but finished 41st. "He earned the only thing that has ever eluded him, and I raced in the Daytona 500. I know I won't forget it, Dale won't forget it, and I'm sure the fans will never forget it."

CHAPTER 19

KYLE PETTY

Petty's package: First third-generation driver to win at NASCAR Winston Cup level; first win came at Richmond in 1986 with Wood Brothers; in 1992 and 1993 finished a career-best fifth in the season standings; won pole position for 1993 Daytona 500; ended 1997 season with four top-fives in five races.

Sure, drivers like Dale Earnhardt Jr. and Jason Jarrett know what life in the shadows is like, having fathers who are NASCAR living legends. Imagine how Kyle Petty must feel—his father, "King" Richard Petty, is THE all-time NASCAR legend.

Petty, born on June 2, 1960, and now living in North Carolina, does not mind that people think he is a rebel with his long hair and earrings. At the same time, he claims his father had a similar image for a bygone era. So Petty believes his father has no problem with the earrings and long hair.

"It's not that he has any conflicts—he was different, when you really get into it," Petty said. "Hey, I don't say anything about him wearing cowboy hats and boots. How many guys from North

Carolina wear cowboy boots and dark glasses, and at night! We are a really close family; he has three sisters, and they're all around here. It's been a great thing to have the family so involved in the same profession. It's been a positive thing 100 percent."

Although his father is the "King," Petty never felt any pressure.

"I probably should, but I don't think I ever let it bother me," Petty said. "And I won't start now. Really, though, I enjoy the driving part so much, just being in a race car running around in circles, I guess, that I never really paid much attention to the pressure side of it."

Not that Petty always paid attention to what his father said— like many other kids, Petty had to learn things on his own.

"He said, 'I can tell you everything you need to know, but you're not going to believe me until you hit the wall hard three or four times,'" Petty recalls. "When I was 19 years old, I thought I was smarter than Einstein and more invincible than Superman, so I wasn't doing much listening to anybody. So basically he let me go out there on my own and learn, then get back to him after a while and then ask some questions. That was the only way it was going to work, I guess."

Petty's roots in racing actually go one generation deeper: His grandfather (Richard's dad) Lee Petty founded Petty Enterprises in 1949.

"It seems like yesterday I was watching my daddy drive on the beach course at Daytona," said Richard Petty. "There's a lot of history at Petty Enterprises. We're proud of what we've done."

Lee Petty won 55 races and two NASCAR championships as a driver before relinquishing full-time driving duties.

"I tell ya, my grandfather raced, my father raced, and when I got ready and told my father I wanted to race, he was switching from Chrysler to Chevy, so he gave me an old Dodge and said, 'Here it is, go race it,'" Petty said. "So I went to Daytona and never looked back."

Richard entered politics at one point, winning an election as a county official. Don't expect to see Petty seeking office any time soon.

"I don't think North Carolina is quite ready for a long-haired, earring-wearing secretary of state or governor," Petty said with a smile. "Or even a county commissioner for that matter. So I'll have to give politics a second thought some other time. I'll have to leave that to the rest of the family. I look at it as if I'm about 14 or 15. I'm still young enough that I like Hot Wheels and like to play with them, yet old enough that I like to go out and have a good time."

Petty has also done some broadcast work on the side, often offering commentary for Busch Grand National races. It's something he enjoys.

"I really do," Petty said. "It's been a nice sideline to my driving, and it's something that seems to come pretty naturally. I tell ya, it's a lot harder than it looks, that's for sure."

While Petty has witnessed the growth of NASCAR firsthand, even he admits to being amazed at the nonstop surge in the sport's popularity.

"I find it to be surprising—not the growth itself, though," Petty said. "The last seven or eight years have been amazing. As far as it being the No. 1 sport in America, I think we all knew that, but we were just waiting for it to catch on."

Petty and his wife, Pattie, have two sons, Adam and Austin, and a daughter, Montgomery Lee.

Petty lists collecting Elvis memorabilia, listening to country music, shopping and golfing as his hobbies. He also rides a Harley-Davidson motorcycle, and he used that hobby for a good cause, starting a charity ride that many other NASCAR stars participate in.

"The idea came at about 3 o'clock one morning out in the middle of the Arizona desert going to Phoenix," Petty said. "I ride with a bunch of my friends to races and that's where the idea came from. We do just one charity ride a year, and it has really grown to be a popular thing that does a lot of good."

In 1993, Petty was fifth in the Winston Cup points standings when he had 15 top-10 finishes (he was also fifth in 1992). Petty was 15th in the Winston Cup points standings in 1994, and finished in the same spot for the 1997 season.

Petty drove for the Felix Sabates team from 1989 to the end of the 1996 season. While some driver-owner splits are acrimonious, this one was just the opposite.

"Petty has become like a son to me over the past eight years, and we have enjoyed many personal accomplishments together," Sabates said when Petty left to join PE2. "We have a lot of mutual respect and love for one another, and I know that Felix Sabates will continue to be a winning organization and Kyle Petty will continue to be a winning (NASCAR) Winston Cup driver."

Petty echoed those sentiments.

"This is just one of those things that happens to everyone at one point or another," said Petty. "We have had a lot of great years, but our time together has run its course."

After several years with many different teams, Petty returned to Petty Enterprises—PE2 is his team's ownership title—in 1997.

"One night about 2 a.m., I was out riding on my motorcycle and just decided to start my own team," he said. "That's when I started talking to my father and organizing a team I could be comfortable with and that could be comfortable with me."

A new team does not mean lower goals.

"It's a goal for every team to win, whether it's your inaugural season or your 50th," Petty said. "That's a really, really high goal for us. We're working toward that every week."

Petty also wanted to make sure he continued his family's hands-on involvement with Winston Cup racing.

"Family is the answer," Petty said. "My father has his own team. I have two sons, Adam and Austin, and I just wanted to build something myself that I could combine with Petty Enterprises where we could run a few cars together. My grandfather started this whole deal, and I want to keep the tradition alive. . . so who knows, maybe they (Adam and Austin) will take it to the fourth generation."

His father said the move made sense all the way around.

"From a business standpoint this makes a lot of sense," said seven-time NASCAR Winston Cup Series champion Richard Petty. "But from a personal standpoint, or a family point of view, this makes even more sense."

"I guess I'm proof that you can go home again," Petty said. "People have been asking me for years when I would return to Petty Enterprises. I didn't really have a master plan when the season started, but the pieces fell into place quickly. It felt like the right thing to do."

Richard's influence on Petty's life will always be prominent.

"I go to him a lot," Petty said. "As far as racing, there's not much he doesn't know, so if I want the best answers I go to the best. But our relationship is multilayered. He's really good about not letting business stuff mix with family stuff. If I spend too much money, I can still go over at Christmas, and he gives me a present."

Petty also likes the fact that his family's operation is all under the same roof, one that extends back nearly half a century.

"Growing up, I didn't really pay attention to the history stuff of our family that much," Petty said. "But I guess I'm gaining perspective as I grow older. Being a dad and raising a family makes you appreciate your own background."

Kyle Petty actually started his career at Petty Enterprises, and in his debut won an ARCA race at Daytona in 1979. Back then, on Feb. 12, 1979, Petty hopped behind the wheel of that Dodge and drove onto the track at Daytona. A couple of hours later, Petty, who had not even run at a local track, was in Victory Lane at the ARCA Daytona 200.

By 1981, Petty had joined his father full time on the Winston Cup circuit. Four years later, he won his first Winston Cup race in Richmond, Virginia, when he was with the Wood Brothers. He stayed there until after the 1988 season. Then he had two NASCAR Winston Cup Series wins over a period of four seasons. In 1989, Kyle formed his relationship with Felix Sabates.

Petty drives in the No. 44 Hot Wheels car. The logical match between Hot Wheels and NASCAR is furthered by the third-generation Petty behind the wheel.

"So far I've gotten some cool racetracks. I gave John Andretti's son one and Ward Burton's son one," Petty said. "In fact, we were playing with them at Darlington. I've got one of every car they've got, and I still have my old ones from when I was a kid. You can't forget about the old ones. It's really been a lot of fun."

Mattel was delighted to hook up with NASCAR and the Pettys.

"The Hot Wheels/Petty team is a powerful combination of the top name in motorsports with the largest vehicle manufacturer in the world," said Jim Wagner, vice president of marketing and licensing for Mattel. "Hot Wheels has dominated the toy vehicle business for the past 28 years, and its partnership with the legendary Petty family, with over 47 years of racing experience, is a unique and exciting opportunity to bring entire families to the sport of stock car racing."

Hot Wheels ended up with Petty in a roundabout way.

"It's a long story," Petty said, "but basically, when I announced I was leaving SABCO, they sent out some feelers for a Winston Cup team and made it clear they were very interested in coming to Winston Cup racing. Jack Baldwin, who used to drive their IMSA car, helped it along. And so through Jack, and through the grace of God, that's how I ended up with them. It's great to find a sponsor like Hot Wheels that shares those (family) values. It's a pretty cool deal.

"I finally found a sponsor that fits my personality because Hot Wheels is the world's coolest car company," Petty said. "I'm just a grown-up kid at heart. I played with Hot Wheels when I was younger. Now, I'm still playing with Hot Wheels, just bigger in size. This is a super deal, and I'm looking forward to being associated with the Hot Wheels name."

While many drivers go through a routine before each race, Petty really is not superstitious.

"The only ritual I have before each race is every morning, whether my family is at the track or at home, we say a prayer before the race," Petty said. "Or Max Helton will come by my car, and he and I will say a prayer before we get started. That's about it."

When it comes to a favorite track, one can't get an answer from Petty. Rather, he's so familiar with all of the different venues that he likes them all for different reasons.

"My standard answer is, after you've run them for 10 or 15 years, you enjoy all of them, and you learn to look forward to each and every one," Petty said.

Now that Petty is a veteran of the sport, he is often asked how long before he retires.

"I don't know—until I don't enjoy it anymore," Petty said. "And right now I love nothing more than to get into a race car. I'll be like my father. The day I wake up and I don't enjoy it anymore then I'll quit."

Truth be told, Petty is a veteran driver. At the same time, people think since he's been around for so long, he must be at least 50. But he started in 1979 at the young age of 18. So while he's among the truly veteran drivers, he's only a half-dozen years older than some of the older rookies.

"Most people assume I'm older than I really am because of how early I started," Petty said. "When you look at me, you think, 'God, he's been here 100 years.' It used to amaze me to hear people talk about the younger drivers in our sport. Those guys were 32, 34 years old—older than me at the time—but they were considered the 'young lions.'"

In November of 1997, Petty—only 37 at the time—made his 500th career Winston Cup Series start.

"Five hundred career starts? That's hard to believe, ain't it?" Petty said. "I guess I'm old. Starting your 500th career race is a neat deal, but Terry Labonte had 500 consecutive starts and is still going (567 to be exact). Now that's a big deal. Five hundred races ain't a big deal. Well, maybe it is; it means I've been here longer than I should have been."

The 500 race total is impressive, but don't think Petty has a particular number in mind.

"I'm not shooting for nothing," Petty said. "If I was shooting for 1,000 starts, I wouldn't have sat out all those races when I could have been in a race car. It's just like when I broke my leg. I sat out for six months on purpose. I could have come back probably after three months, but then I'd be limping like Bill Elliott and Darrell

Waltrip. I didn't want to limp the rest of my life. That's why I didn't come back too soon. Then, in '88, when I went to drive for Felix, we only ran a limited schedule that year. If I'd have been concerned about things like this, I would have started my 500th race last season or the tail end of the season before that. . . you know how it is in racing. You're only as good as you were last week. It makes it a lot better when you can say the last month of the year you ran good, so you can have something to look forward to next year."

One of Petty's goals now, in addition to winning, is building a top-flight two-car program with his father.

"I look at it a couple of different ways," Petty said. "If there is pressure now, it's the pressure I put on myself. There's no pressure from Hot Wheels; they've been incredibly good for a first-time sponsor in Winston Cup racing. Do I put pressure on myself? Am I tough? Do I think I can drive a race car? Yes, to all of those questions. Can I win races with this team? Yes. I would like to build this into a competitive team like my father's—we'd have two competitive teams then. I may be the owner at some point of Petty Enterprises and PE2. Then, if people ask, 'Were you a success?' I'll ask them, 'As an owner or a driver?' The way to judge what makes a team a success is the long term, not two or three years. Let's talk in 10 or 15 years, and if I'm still around with it, yes, it should be a success."

A career in music was an option at one time. But when it came right down to it, the choice to pick racing wasn't that difficult.

"I loved my other career, but there came a time when I had to choose music or racing because each takes a lot of time to do right," Petty said. "So I had to take my focus back to racing 100 percent. I miss music a bit, sure. But racing is my life."

CHAPTER 20

ROBERT PRESSLEY

Pressley's impressions: Was 1987 Winston Racing Series Mid-Atlantic champion; had 16 wins and 27 top-fives in 29 races; repeated title the following year with 13 wins and 29 top-fives in 36 races; runner-up to Ricky Craven in Winston Cup Rookie of the Year competition in 1995.

"It's a good time to be Robert Pressley. This team has been so good to work with," Robert Pressley said. "Everyone has made such an effort to help make this team a success. I can't wait for next year to get started."

Pressley was referring to himself in the third person because he had just signed deals to run on both the Winston Cup and Busch Grand National Series for the 1998 season. A lot of hard work and dedication had put Pressley right where he wanted to be.

And what a distance he has traveled—both literally and figuratively—in his racing career.

Pressley's father is short track legend Bob Pressley. Robert was a standout at short tracks near his home in Asheville, North Carolina, as he won short track titles at the New Asheville Speedway and at South Carolina's Greenville-Pickens Speedway.

Pressley got into the Busch Series by forming a team with co-owner Brad Daugherty, who played for the Cleveland Cavaliers in the NBA.

It was just a few years ago—1985 to be exact—when Pressley was battling Ricky Craven for the Winston Cup Rookie of the Year honors. Pressley, with only three Winston Cup starts to his name, had taken over Harry Gant's ride. But Craven would win Rookie of the Year when, in the final race of the season, Pressley's engine had problems, and he finished 41st.

Pressley bounced around with the No. 33 and No. 29 in 1996 and 1997 and finished the season in the No. 77 Jasper Engines/Federal-Mogul team.

Although Pressley didn't make it to the top of the Winston Cup heat right away, he did make great strides, especially in the later half of the season.

"Our goals have been the same since the start of the season," said Pressley, who was born June 2, 1960, and whose hobbies include landscaping, gardening and listening to music. "We want to become a top-20 race team, week in and week out. We want to take care of qualifying on the first day for the rest of the year. We want to be able to run competitively with different setups and at different tracks. We want to be realistic about what we can do and finish in the top 25 in the points."

Still, having a signed contract to drive in the Winston Cup Series was an emotional boost after bouncing around for a couple of years under a cloud of uncertainty.

"It is nice for me—it is the first time in my career I haven't been in the rumor mill, you know, the July-August time of the year," Pressley said. "We are not a threat to win a Winston Cup championship, but we are becoming more than just a car that shows up now."

Winning takes a lot of ingredients.

"It takes a chemistry," Pressley said. "And I think the chemistry is getting closer between the driver, owner and crew chief. We are trying to build this team one day at a time, not just taking a leap. We are doing it bit by bit, sort of sneaking up on it, and we are going to become one of the 10 best teams, we hope."

Pressley once had his brother as his crew chief. It's a scenario he envisions happening again in the future, perhaps.

"We have talked about it; there are some things he and I would like to do," Pressley said. "There has been talk that he and I would look at getting back together down the road. More than likely, if it was to happen, it would happen in the next few years."

Pressley has adapted well to having a teammate—and that teammate is none other than Rick Mast.

"We share all our data in testing, and we go through all the notes we have from the race we ran, and the race we have coming up," Pressley said. "So, it's been a real good thing for Jasper Motorsports."

While the time demands are unbearable in some ways, Pressley has made it more bearable by keeping his family with him most of the time.

"We have a schedule that is not as bad on us as you might think," Pressley said. "I am gone from home an average of six days a week, but the family is there with me four days a week. They come in on Thursday night. We stay in the family coach at the racetrack. And I really get more time with them when I am racing than when I am off and testing for a weekend. Then I don't hardly see them."

"Relaxing" to Pressley simply means spending some time at home with his wife and their children.

"We just get back to the house. I have a little land up there," Pressley said. "It's not a farm or anything, but I have some work to do; I have some tractors. I don't golf or fish. I enjoy landscaping and working with the land. When I relax, it's usually doing something like riding around on heavy equipment and working at home."

Pressley's father has raced for more than three decades, and it was a family affair in the Pressley household.

"My dad has been racing, and still is racing, for 34 years," Pressley said. "That's all we've done since I can remember—three brothers and a sister, hanging around a racetrack. Until I was about 15 years old, I thought everybody's dad raced. My brothers are in racing, my sister married a race car driver. I never thought about doing anything else or wanted to do anything else."

NASCAR legend Harry Gant gave Pressley plenty of direction. "My friendship with Harry started before my Winston Cup career started," Pressley said. "We've known each other for years; he raced with my dad back in the late '70s and early '80s. He really helped excel my Busch Series career—he was a big help. I think that relationship really helped me, as far as when he was going to retire, he got to choose who he wanted in there. He traveled with us that first year, and that was my best year in Winston Cup, before this year. I don't see Harry much. I miss him a lot because he really helped me a lot when I started out."

Pressley likes almost all of the drivers on the tour, something that makes his job more enjoyable.

"Probably 95 percent of 'em are best friends," Pressley said. "But Rick Mast and I have been friends since our Skoal days when we were teammates. I can ask Rick anything about the race car or the track or anything on or off the track. And another guy who's really been good to me like Harry was is Mark Martin. He'll really shoot you straight. If he doesn't want to tell you something, he'll just say, 'I can't tell you.' But when he does tell you something, it's a straight shot."

While Pressley has a lot of NASCAR memories, two stand out.

"It has to be two races. It has to be both Darlington Busch Grand National wins," Pressley said. "In one of them we beat Harry Gant on the last lap. The next year he ran second to us again, but we beat him all day long. The first one was just a one-lap race. But the next year, to come back and beat the man who was the best there was at Darlington, those were my two most memorable moments in NASCAR."

Pressley also placed 13th in the ACDelco 400 at the North Carolina Motor Speedway in 1997.

"What a race!" Pressley said after the event. "The guys did one heck of a job in the pits all day long. I was real proud of the job they did in the pit crew competition. I think we could have been in the top 10, but we're real happy running all day today and finishing in the top 15. We needed this bad. This is a big confidence booster for the guys."

Pressley appreciated his team's perseverance during the 1998 season. Even a 20th-place finish was good in March 1998 in the TranSouth Financial 400, because Pressley had to overcome an air-gun failure and a stuck throttle. The points moved him up from 34th to 32nd in the points standings at the time.

"We really had to work hard to get this one," Pressley said. "The car was really good. We didn't make a chassis change all day. We went up a half-pound one time on air pressure, and that was about it. I think we had about a 12th-place car. . . we just didn't get the breaks we needed to keep it there."

Disaster struck again on March 30 at Bristol when a power steering failure caused him to go hard into the wall at the Food City 500 with just 10 laps left.

"The power steering started acting up with about 125 laps left, and I had been fighting the car just trying to hang on," Pressley said. "After that last restart, I headed down into Turn 3, and the car just kept going straight. I locked it down, but it still hit pretty hard. I hurt from my bellybutton on up."

Pressley started the No. 77 Jasper Engines & Transmissions Ford in the 31st position. But because of great pit stops at Bristol, he was up to sixth place.

"The guys have really been working hard on pit stops lately, and it started paying off," Pressley said. "We were able to stay right with the lead pack of cars, even though we were pitted on the backstretch, and that doesn't happen without some good pitwork.

"We were right there," Pressley said. "We had a top-10 car. The crew performed like a top-10 team all weekend long. From the time the car rolled off the truck for practice to each pit stop during the race, we were there."

A broken A-frame resulted in a 31st-place for Pressley on April 27 at Talladega.

"We had maybe a top-10 or top-15 car today," Pressley said at the time. "I had plenty of power, and the car was performing well. I could really move up through the field. That broken shock mount just threw us a curve."

Finally, in early May at the California 500, Pressley was back in his groove, taking 17th place.

"The drivetrain was very strong and the fuel mileage was excellent," Pressley said. "The car was tight during the race, but I'm proud of the way the crew worked to loosen it up. They really hung in there to give us a respectable finish."

Pressley followed that effort with a 12th-place finish in the Winston Open.

However, Pressley's Busch Grand National efforts have spoken volumes about the kind of driver he is, and he still enjoys running on the Busch circuit—when the schedule allows.

When Pressley won back-to-back spring races at Darlington, he became the only NASCAR Busch Series regular to win more than one time at the track drivers say is "Too Tough to Tame."

"I don't understand why, but I seem to do better on the really difficult tracks," Pressley said. "Darlington is a difficult place to drive because there's trouble all the way around the place. The walls come up on you very quickly, and you have to keep a very high level of concentration or you'll wind up in trouble. And sometimes, even when you're doing everything right, Darlington has a way of jumping out and getting you. Darrell Waltrip once said you never beat Darlington; it just waits for another time to get you. That pretty much says it all. It's a driver's track."

Although some tracks look alike, all are quite different.

"If you look at their pictures, Charlotte, Texas and Atlanta all look alike," Pressley said. "But in reality, they're all three very different."

Louden is another special track.

"The thing about New Hampshire is it has a great racetrack and some of the greatest fans in the world," Pressley said. "When you make a trip like this, you realize it goes against all the stereotypes you've heard about stock car racing. This sport isn't regional. The roots may be in the South, but its popularity reaches out to every corner of the country—and further."

Bristol—the short track that will produce a reaction from any driver just by mentioning the name—is also a tough course to conquer.

"It takes a lot more than speed to be successful at Bristol," Pressley said. "It's a track that demands the most out of a car and the driver. It's probably the most demanding track on the Busch Series circuit. If you've got a fast car and if running 100 mph down the straightaways a couple inches from the next guy doesn't bother you, then Bristol's for you. Bristol's one of my favorite tracks, and I know it's one of the race team's favorite tracks."

Since he was among the top 35 in the Winston Cup points standings, Pressley no longer was eligible for a provisional in the Busch Series. Ironically, he likes the challenge that the rule brings to him as a regular on both circuits.

"It proves why NASCAR is the best sport in the world," Pressley said. "You have to be so perfect to make the show. A little bobble during qualifying, something that took less time than a light turning on, is all it took. It proves just how competitive the racing at this level has become."

His Busch crew chief said the format provides a tough test each time.

"Qualifying is nerve-racking," crew chief Steve Plattenberger said. "Since our driver's in the top 35 in points in the Winston Cup Series, we're not eligible for a provisional (in the Busch Series). And since a lot of our qualifying is one day, one lap, it puts a lot of pressure on the team and the driver. We don't have any room for mistakes. There's no margin for error. We either do it right one time, or we go home. It's a tough way to have to survive in this business."

While his crew chief deals with the nerves, Pressley handles the driving in a calm manner.

"I think the best way to get prepared for any race is to take it in stride," Pressley said. "You have to keep everything in perspective.

Just because this race will have a lot of people and a big purse, it doesn't change the way you go about getting ready."

Even though Pressley was having a rough ride for the first part of the 1998 season in his Busch car, he came back and won the pole at Hickory in April.

Pressley was especially happy to get back in the No. 59 Kingsford Matchlite car after being forced to miss several races during the 1998 Winston Cup season because the races had conflicting dates and/or locations.

"It's good to be back with the Kingsford car," Pressley said. "It's a lot of fun to be in a car that's competitive every week. We had a great run at California last year. We led some laps and finished fifth."

Running both series can take a toll on a driver, both physically and mentally.

"People don't realize how demanding a race schedule can be, but when you're trying to do two different series, it gets really tough," Pressley said. "I know it puts everyone in a bind on both circuits, but ST Motorsports has an advantage over most other teams—its preparation. When you have good people and good race cars, it makes it easier to tackle the difficult situations."

Still, having the guaranteed ride was nice for Pressley, who enjoys the Busch Grand National Series.

"It's good to be back with the race team for a long stretch," Pressley said. "It's difficult being away from this race team. There's a tremendous atmosphere with this race team, and they produce some of the best cars in racing. Maybe I can give them some good runs. Now that we have a chance to build some continuity in the next couple months, we can get to that next level that leads to wins. Winning is contagious. Once you win, it's all you want."

ELLIOTT SADLER

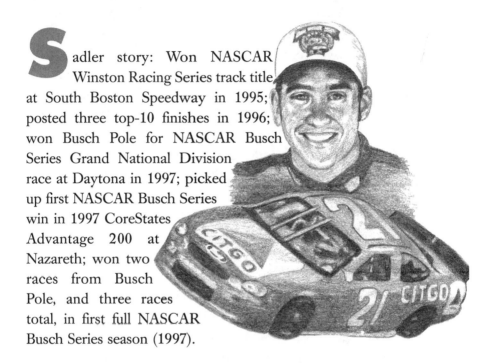

Sadler story: Won NASCAR Winston Racing Series track title at South Boston Speedway in 1995; posted three top-10 finishes in 1996; won Busch Pole for NASCAR Busch Series Grand National Division race at Daytona in 1997; picked up first NASCAR Busch Series win in 1997 CoreStates Advantage 200 at Nazareth; won two races from Busch Pole, and three races total, in first full NASCAR Busch Series season (1997).

Elliott Sadler is in high gear, and the young phenom will shift again—even higher—as he heads to the Winston Cup series in 1999 in the No. 21 Citgo Ford Taurus.

"Winston Cup is a tough level, mentally and physically," said Sadler, who was born April 30, 1975. "We were just kind of shopping around a little bit. My dream has always been to make it to Winston Cup. We were looking to try to do it with Diamond Ridge next year (in 1999), and sponsors just never evolved. I do want to say right now on the record that Gary Bechtel has been unbelievably nice to me and has given me a great opportunity, but we just could never get things worked out. The Wood Brothers came along, and that's a great race team. If you talk to everybody in the garage, they talk about how nice a team it is. The history behind that team, looking at them with David Pearson and the races they've won and the legendary status that team has got, I think it's great for me to be associated with somebody like that. So that was a big part of it."

"We are looking forward to having Elliott in our program," said team co-owner and crew chief Eddie Wood. "He has proven himself to be a smart, patient and talented driver in the Busch Series, and we believe he will have great success in Winston Cup racing."

Sadler started his Busch Grand National career in 1995 at South Boston Speedway, a familiar track as he ran several years there in the NASCAR Late Model Stock Car competition. He won the NASCAR Winston Racing Series track title at SBS in 1995.

In October of 1998, Sadler came away with the win at the ACDelco 200 at Rockingham, and his older brother, Hermie, finished third.

"This is a great day for all of us in the Sadler family," Sadler said in Victory Lane. "We're just happy to finish the season on a good, strong note. Hopefully, this will give me momentum for next year. The changes we made on the pit stops were good and that was the key."

Sadler started way back in the 19th spot at Rockingham. "I think it's the biggest win of my life," Sadler said. "The last few races, we have been struggling at the shop. We fell behind, and we got the car right for the last little shootout. It's a great win; the biggest win of my life. The longer we ran there at the end, the better it got, and the bigger my smile got. To win at Rockingham was great."

Another big win came in the city that is home to the famous Gateway Arch.

"St. Louis was the inaugural event, but a win's a win, and my name will always be in the record books. There were a lot of Winston Cup guys there, and it was a 300-mile race," Sadler said. "It was a big boost for me and the whole team."

Winning the pole at Daytona was also big. "It was unreal to go to a big track, all the hype and the prestige that goes along with that," he said. "To sit on the pole that whole week and get the press and the things like that was a big boost to my career. And it was a big boost to my confidence. I could say, 'Elliott, this is a big track, but you can do it.'"

The superspeedways and the "drafting" provide drivers with a challenge and concern they don't get on short tracks or road courses.

"I look forward to running Talladega because I need more drafting experience," said Sadler. "It is like a chess game. You have to contemplate the effect it would have on your car. If you don't make the right move, you can go backwards real quick."

Sadler also believes starting on the pole can give a driver an edge.

"I think starting from the pole gives you several advantages," Sadler said. "First, if you're starting up front you're less likely to get caught up in an accident than if you started farther back in the field. It also gives the entire team a confidence and a morale boost when you win a pole. It lets the driver and the team know they have a good enough car to win the race. When your team has that confidence going into a race, it shows in the team's performance when it comes to racing and pit stops."

Other tracks are also interesting.

"Darlington is one of my favorite tracks to run," Sadler said. "From a driver's standpoint it is really a challenge, which is one of the reasons I look forward to racing there. It really tests my skills.

"Darlington is a pretty tough place to try and get around. Success there depends a lot on having a good car and a lot of horsepower, but after a point the driver really has to take over. At Darlington, the cars run right up against the wall, and it can get pretty tricky in Turns 3 and 4. All of those extra elements are what makes Darlington a great place to race.

"Michigan was the first track I raced on that was really big, and experience-wise, it was unreal," Sadler said. "It was a little scary at first, but now I actually look forward to racing on the big tracks. Even though this isn't the type of track I cut my teeth on, I really look forward to racing on them."

Racing with Hermie is something Sadler enjoys, especially in 1998 as teammates.

"We've raced go-karts and things for a long time. I'm just glad that Gary Bechtel has given us a chance to be teammates at such a high level of racing, this Busch Series," Sadler said.

Bechtel saw Sadler's talent long ago.

"Elliott Sadler is one heck of a nice guy, and I've enjoyed watching him develop into a top-notch race car driver over the past year," said Bechtel, owner of Diamond Ridge Motorsports. "Elliott was a young driver when we brought him on board, but we could see his potential to go a long way in this sport."

Sadler has been racing for quite some time.

"I started when I was 7 years old. I raced go-karts up and down the East Coast," Sadler said. "A guy named Danny Wyatt got us into it. We flipped the kart three times at Broadneck Speedway, and I cried all the way home because I didn't get to finish the race. We went on to race until I was 18 years old when I started racing Late Model cars. I started them in 1993 until I started running in Busch racing."

So one of Sadler's biggest racing influences is Hermie. "It would have to be my brother," Sadler said. "Little brothers are always looking up to older brothers in all sports, not just racing. When he was running Late Models, I was always hanging around trying to help. It's kind of neat when a family member is your biggest influence. It's really done a lot for me and the big family presence that NASCAR has."

The biggest influences on his racing career include other family members.

"Probably my uncle, Bud Elliott, and my daddy—they both raced back in the '70s at local tracks around Virginia and North Carolina," Sadler said. "I think racing was born into my blood; I don't think I had any choice. There's a lot of racing in our family. So, my biggest influence was mostly my family members themselves."

Other family members are also involved with his career. "My dad started racing in the '70s," Sadler said. "My mama and daddy are at every single race. It's great to have the family involved; it makes it very special for both Hermie and me."

Sadler made history himself, picking up a win at Bristol, but admits his hometown-area tracks also are held close to his heart.

"Richmond is very special to Hermie and me because it's right there at home and a lot of our friends and family can watch," Sadler said. "But I'd have to say Bristol is a favorite track. Not because we won there, but Bristol has always been a place I enjoyed watching races. And now to compete there—that's a race I always keep highlighted on the schedule."

His strong background in the shop has also helped him in the standings.

"I think so, because I grew up working on my race cars and setting them up," Sadler said. "I participate 100 percent on setting the cars up. I feel like when I get to the track, since I know what's under the car, I know how to fix it."

While he puts in countless shop hours, he also understands the role of going on the road and testing at various tracks.

"Testing is very important because not only does it get you secluded track time, but you can try so many different things that you don't have time to do on race weekends," Sadler said. "On race weekends you get two hours, and with 40 cars out there, you don't always get a clean lap. Testing not only helps you at that racetrack, but at others, too."

Don't think for a moment that his extended resumé will ever bear the label of owner/driver.

"I saw what my brother went through, and that isn't anything I'd want to do," Sadler said. "I like going to the shop, but wouldn't want to deal with the hiring and the paperwork. I like the driving; I want to keep myself as far away from the desk stuff as I can."

Growing up, Sadler had his share of favorites. Come 1999, he will race against many of them, as he has in the Busch series facing greats like Dale Jarrett and Mark Martin.

"I've always been a Dale Earnhardt fan. I guess where I'm from, that part of Virginia, everyone's an Earnhardt fan. He's one driver who, if he's getting paid one dime or one million, he's going to race hard," Sadler said. "I always liked Benny Parsons. Now that I've raced against a lot of them, Mark Martin, Jeff Burton and Dale Jarrett have helped me a lot. After being involved in racing, I really admire what those guys do. After practicing a Cup car, I really admire what those guys drive, going three-wide at those speeds."

Although Sadler is young, he is experienced.

"Even though I'm young, I feel like I've been racing a long time," Sadler said. "Percentage-wise, I've been racing 60 or 70 percent of my life. But I hope to stay in the sport as long as I can."

While Hermie is on the BGN series, Sadler has lots of other friends.

"I'd say Randy LaJoie, Buckshot Jones, Mike McLaughlin and my brother, of course," Sadler said. "I try to be friends with all of them. Randy and I always play golf, so I have to say he's a good friend. I have such a great time racing, and just being around those guys each weekend is fun."

Sadler knows the demands on his time will continue to grow, but he loves meeting the fans.

"I think a lot of the time demands are off the track with the sponsors and the media," he said. "It's pretty easy in that car if you're used to it. It's been tough on me to relate to the media, but I love meeting the fans and talking with all of them. I try to do that the best I can. I love the fans and signing autographs. The more I do of that, the better it makes me feel. And that's why I love being a part of this NASCAR family."

While he races full time, Sadler believes aspiring drivers should still do well in school.

"I went to two years of college, but I left because I was really dedicated to racing," he said. "I was always gone racing, and I didn't get a chance to really get the college experience. But I definitely recommend going to college. However, if you're starting racing, then you should definitely do it yourself. Get in there and get your hands dirty and do it yourself. Whatever it is, in life, in college, or in racing, you should try and do it."

CHAPTER 22

MIKE SKINNER

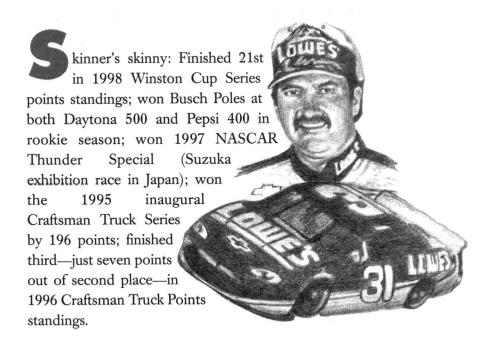

Skinner's skinny: Finished 21st in 1998 Winston Cup Series points standings; won Busch Poles at both Daytona 500 and Pepsi 400 in rookie season; won 1997 NASCAR Thunder Special (Suzuka exhibition race in Japan); won the 1995 inaugural Craftsman Truck Series by 196 points; finished third—just seven points out of second place—in 1996 Craftsman Truck Points standings.

On the way to claiming the first-ever Craftsman Truck Series Championship, Skinner had seven top-five finishes and 18 top-10 finishes in 20 races.

After winning the points championship in the truck series for the 1995 season, Skinner finished third in the truck standings in 1996. He also stepped up in 1996 and made five NASCAR Winston Cup Series starts—he moved up to Winston Cup full time in 1997.

Skinner was the 1997 Rookie of the Year in the Winston Cup Series, winning races in Daytona (just the second rookie to win the Daytona 500 pole), and then at the NASCAR Thunder Special in Japan (not a points race). Skinner had three top-10 finishes in 1997.

"It's a huge accomplishment, and it's an honor," Skinner said. "I don't think we have done anywhere near what we wanted to do, but if you look at the other rookies who are all good racers, it's good to think that we have been at the top of our class."

Skinner's career started long ago, but those memories are still important to him.

"I've been racing forever," Skinner said. "When I got started in racing, I had a '71 Road Runner that had gotten run off the road, and the insurance company totaled it. I bought it back and turned it into a stock car. That was back in . . . well, let's say it was in the late '70s."

Long before he was a star in his own right on the Winston Cup scene, Skinner had heroes that he watched race.

"I think my heroes in racing and the guys who influenced me go back to Richard Petty, Darrell Waltrip—those names come up right off the top of my head," said Skinner, who was born June 28, 1957, and counts golfing, hunting, fishing, riding horses and playing billiards among his hobbies. "Then Tim Richmond came along, and I thought he was a great driver. He was kicking everybody's tails there for a while. I raced Joe Ruttman a lot on the West Coast. I looked up to him as a great competitor. He knew how to win races, and he still does. Of course I have looked up to Dale Earnhardt; most people in this business do. I look up to a lot of people in this business. I guess this is my short list."

Now he works with Dale Earnhardt, driving the No. 31 Lowe's Monte Carlo on the Winston Cup circuit. Working for the Intimidator is not quite intimidating.

"We don't talk too much at the track, but if I need some information about the line or tendencies at the track, Dale has been a great help," Skinner said. "He always takes the time to show me some of the things he knows. All in all, on and off the racetrack, things have gone real well."

Larry McReynolds, who was switched to be Skinner's crew chief midway through 1998 after working as Earnhardt's crew chief, said the two are similar drivers but have different strengths.

"Mike is probably a little more knowledgeable about his race car, his chassis," McReynolds said, "because he works on the cars, and he works on his son's race truck. But obviously, Dale is a great race car driver, and I feel fortunate to have worked with him for a year and a half. And I am looking forward to working with him still at tests and things."

Skinner's driving style is quite similar to that of the Intimidator's.

"The closer our styles are, the more we can benefit ourselves in testing," Skinner said. "With my driving style being like his, what we find out in testing should help the 3 car as well as the 31."

Having Earnhardt as a teammate is something Skinner never imagined being possible.

"It's an honor to have his knowledge and things to draw from," Skinner said.

Being part of a multi-car team is simply the way NASCAR has evolved.

"The reason that they have gone to the multi-car team is that they have twice as much information, twice as much testing— basically, two heads are better than one," Skinner said. "And on the superspeedways, you can team up and help each other earn better spots."

Joining a team with the ultra-competitive Intimidator presented a challenge that Skinner enjoys.

"I think it's better to join a team with expectations and experience and winning ways," Skinner sad. "If you join a rookie team and you're a rookie driver, your success will be very limited. As it is, they expect a lot out of me, and I expect a lot out of them."

Leaving the trucks for the Winston Cup cars was only a small adjustment. The strategy remains the same.

"Basically, driving-wise, there is very little difference," Skinner said. "The adjustment comes from stepping the level of competition up from the truck series to the Winston Cup Series. In the truck series, if you fell back to 20th, it wouldn't be too long before you could get back up there to where you were running. Now in the truck series as well as Winston Cup, if you lose track position, it is awfully hard to get it back because everyone is running the same speed."

The trucks are similar to the Winston Cup cars, according to Skinner. "Actually, the truck has the same weight as the Winston Cup cars," Skinner said. "The only difference is the aerodynamics. The reason the trucks always look loose is the front end's always loose. On new tires you can hardly tell the difference between the truck and the car. After the tires get worn down, then aerodynamically the truck doesn't handle as well as the car. It doesn't have the downforce the car does, and it doesn't maneuver as well as the car."

Skinner is proud that he helped the truck series continue its remarkable growth.

"Without a doubt, I think the NASCAR truck series is here to stay," Skinner said. "The trucks are a lot bigger than their expectations were at this point. The competition is much better. . . And you have a good TV package and NASCAR behind it."

While the Busch Series is known as the "minor" league and the quickest route to the Winston Cup Series, drivers like Skinner and Kenny Irwin Jr., and Rich Bickle show that there's plenty of talent in the truck series who can make the leap to Winston Cup.

"I think it has already proven that it is," Skinner said. "I guess I'm the best example. I think it is a 'proving ground.' You get to race against Winston Cup-caliber teams with Winston Cup-caliber drivers. I'd look for more truck drivers to move up to the Winston Cup instead of Busch."

The truck series provided invaluable experience for Skinner.

"I think the truck series definitely turned my career around and has been extremely positive for some other drivers as well," Skinner said. "It has given so many people a positive experience. And it's wonderful to get so much more out of a racing career than anyone could have dreamed. The hard work has paid off. Although sometimes it feels as if it is not happening soon enough and other times it feels as if it is all rushing by too fast, I am looking forward to a lot more success in my racing career."

Despite wanting to repeat as truck series champion in 1996, it wasn't meant to be for Skinner, who nonetheless claimed the year a victory.

"We were really shocked that we ran as well as we did," Skinner said. "I think our team was even stronger this year. We definitely were within the top three strongest trucks out there. We did everything we needed to do to win this championship, except finish a couple races. There have been championships lost like that before. I remember Rusty Wallace winning nine races and losing the championship. Jeff Gordon won 10 races and lost the championship. We won eight races and lost the championship. We had a broken engine, a couple of accidents and just some plain old-fashioned bad luck that kept us out of it, but I am in no way, shape or form displeased with the year that we had. We were very competitive and ran up front all year. We were in contention to win 20 out of 24 races."

Skinner misses his competitors from the truck days, especially Ron Hornaday and even—something he thought might never happen—Jack Sprague.

"Great driver, hell of a guy off the racetrack—Ron and I have always gotten along well," Skinner said. "Jack and I had a few problems for a while, but toward the end of the season we started to get along well. We actually helped each other on the racetrack some. I really think a lot of both of them."

Although Skinner can't yet claim to be a road course expert, he does enjoy the challenge. Skinner did pick up a road course win in the Craftsman Truck Series and ran well in 1998, holding the lead on a road course in the final 20 laps before being passed by eventual winner Jeff Gordon.

"I love road course racing," Skinner said. "But I'm definitely not a road racer. It's a new challenge, and I love new challenges."

Skinner's always up for a challenge, which is one reason it is hard for him to name one track as his favorite.

"I'll tell you, it's hard for me to have just one favorite racetrack," Skinner said. "Phoenix has always been up there on the top of my list for years, but after racing at the Brickyard, it's hard for any track to compete with that place. The technology they have, the timing devices that tell you exactly how fast you are going through each corner and each straightaway, it's something else. They really stay on top of the racetrack, talking to you every day. And I really like Martinsville, too."

One of the many places where NASCAR has experienced a huge jump in growth is the West Coast. It's a familiar place to Skinner, who started his racing career in California.

"We actually started in northern California, a small half-mile track in Susanville, California," Skinner said. "We started there and moved to asphalt in a few years. We ran in Sacramento, Altamont, Bakersfield, all the short tracks in Northern and Southern California. Then we decided if we were going to make a living, we needed to move to the East Coast. That's how we ended up here."

The influx of higher purses at truck races has helped raise the competition level.

"The more money," Skinner said, "the more side-by-side racing—the more 'hunger' racing. You put up that much money, it's going to be exciting, and if the fans are excited, they'll come."

While the trend seems to be to bigger race venues, Skinner says he hopes NASCAR continues to keep a decent number of short tracks on the docket.

"Basically, I think NASCAR is doing what they have to do," Skinner said. "On the other hand, I'd just as soon race at Martinsville as Talladega. Short tracks are the roots of racing, and I don't know anybody that doesn't like going back to them. But we have huge audiences. And there is nothing worse than a guy who can't get into a race. The sport is growing so fast and so big that they have to grow with it to keep everybody's interest up."

Skinner actually hooked up with Richard Childress in 1992 at the Daytona 500.

"We brought the car down here, and it didn't even have an engine in it," Skinner says of '92. "We rented an engine from Richard Childress, surprisingly enough."

Skinner faded to the background for a while, but didn't abandon his goal of being a regular in one of NASCAR's top series. "I just never gave up," Skinner said. "I think that's the whole key to this stuff, to just not give up. If I'd have given up, I'd have never been happy. I wanted to run Winston Cup. That was my dream."

When NASCAR started the truck series in 1995 and Childress was convinced to enter a team, he thought of who would drive for him, and immediately Skinner came to mind.

"I knew he had a lot of potential," Childress says. "He was the kind of driver I wanted."

In 1997—his rookie season on the Winston Cup after running just a handful of races during the 1996 season—Skinner took the pole at Daytona.

"This is unbelievable. I don't know if my feelings are explainable," Skinner told reporters at the time. "We came real close to winning a pole at Phoenix last year, and I thought it would have been neat to have done it and gotten into the Busch Clash. I thought at the time maybe we could do it this year, but I never expected this."

"It was a pretty spectacular thing for us, especially with Mike being a rookie and myself not ever having that great a success at a superspeedway," said Kevin Hamlin, Skinner's crew chief at the time (Hamlin took over as Dale Earnhardt's crew chief during the 1998 season).

The pole came despite a potentially costly miscue by Skinner before he even hit the track.

"I made a big-time rookie mistake," Skinner said. "When I left pit road I went out of first gear and put it in fourth gear and just about killed the motor. I went around and took the green and there was debris on the track. I thought somebody must have cut a tire or something, so I drove around it. Driving around it might have helped the car. It got a little bit loose, and I heard that old motor free up. I thought, 'This could be good.'"

When Hamlin joined Childress' organization specifically to be the crew chief for Skinner during the 1997 season, he knew little about his driver.

"Richard asked me if I had ever seen Mike race, and I told him I had only watched a truck race here and there, so I hadn't paid a lot of attention," Hamlin said. "He said, 'Well, just kind of watch him,' and I got more and more impressed every time I did. It's unbelievable what he can do with a truck or car or whatever he happens to be sitting in. He's got a tremendous amount of talent."

Skinner gave his teammate—Earnhardt—a boost at the Daytona 500 to start the 1998 season, and Earnhardt ended a long Daytona drought with a win, something he pushed part of the credit for onto Skinner, who was just glad to help out.

"At Daytona, everything has to be just right," Skinner said. "I told someone the other day that it seems like if you buckle your seat belts the wrong way you could lose a tenth of a second."

Before Daytona, Skinner cut his proverbial racing teeth at his hometown area tracks.

At Susanville Speedway in California, Skinner won six races in 1976, his first year there. The following year, he won 12 of 14 races and won the track championship.

"When I first started, we would race hard and then go out and party hard," Skinner said. "Then, in my second or third year, I started realizing I might be able to do this for a living, and my goals changed. My dreams of running Winston Cup started."

Someone with whom Skinner competed in California, Terry Elledge, had established himself as a top engine builder. In 1983, Elledge got a huge break when he was hired to run Petty Enterprises' engine shop. Elledge pressed Skinner to come along to the East Coast.

"He just had a magic touch with a car," Elledge says. "So I said, 'The only way you're ever going to make it in racing is to be on the East Coast.'"

Skinner is the father of two, Jaime and Dustin, with his wife, Beth, who played a big role in whether to move all the way across the country.

"Beth finally said, 'Look, if you're gonna do it, let's go. If not, be satisfied with where you're at,'" Skinner recalled. "So we loaded up and came East."

Through his connection with Elledge, Skinner worked in Petty's engine department doing odd jobs, one of which was grinding cylinder blocks.

The story only continues to get better from there. After a year with Petty's group, Skinner joined Cliff Stewart's NASCAR Winston Cup team, working as a tire changer and fabricator for Rusty Wallace, who was a rookie that season.

Though he had made the big-time—the Winston Cup Series—Skinner was discontent. He wanted to be part of the game behind the wheel, not changing one.

"By the end of that year, I got to thinking this was not why I came here," Skinner said. "I was helping Rusty's career, not my own. I had won a lot of races out West, and this wasn't doing me any good. I quit working for race teams and went into business, opened a body shop. I just started running Late Model cars, whatever I could run."

From there, Skinner got a shot at driving Late Models at Caraway Speedway near Asheboro, North Carolina, and then he bought a Winston Cup Series car in 1986 from Cecil Gordon. Skinner made the field in his first try, at Martinsville, and finished 22nd.

After running two more Winston Cup races that year, Skinner ran out of money.

"There just wasn't any money there," Skinner said. "It was too hard to compete with no money and no people, no full-time help at all. I went to Rockingham (in '87) and missed the race, and it took me two years to pay the bill. That broke me. That was it. That's when I decided to get a Late Model car."

Skinner headed back to the short tracks in the late 1980s, and in his first season, won 11 of 22 Late Model races. After hooking up with Richard Petty's cousin, Gene Petty, the two swept the Late Model races, winning two track championships and dozens of races. Skinner kept chipping away at getting another NASCAR shot.

"At Gene's, I did a little bit. . . well, mostly everything—fabricating, building cars, being chief cook and bottle washer, sweeping the floors and packing the ice chest," Skinner said. "I just kept working hard. If I had to race Late Model Stock the rest of my life, that's what I'd have done."

From 1990 to '92, Skinner made it into four NASCAR Winston Cup Series races with Dixon's team.

"Mr. Dixon gave me an opportunity to go out and showcase talent," Skinner says. "We knew we didn't have the best equipment, but we made a few races. And we were pretty respectable for a car that had to run used tires after every stop. It obviously was a plus for me to do that. I needed to get in the eyes of the Richard Childresses, the Rick Hendricks, the Jack Roushes and these people, so they could see if I did have any potential."

Jimmy Means, who fielded a car for Skinner in a few races in the '93 and '94 Winston Cup seasons, learned how good Skinner was firsthand, chasing him around the North Carolina Motor Speedway at the 1992 ACDelco 500.

"He drove that thing sideways all day long," Means said. "And to be able to do that at Rockingham, as slick as that racetrack was, I knew there was something there."

Means backed Skinner in the Mountain Dew Southern 500 in 1993 and then again at Rockingham in early '94. Skinner and Petty moved up from the short tracks for a few Busch Series races in 1994. And that's when Skinner started to shine.

Despite driving for a small team with limited means in '94, Skinner won the pole for the Champion Spark Plug 300 Busch Series race, a race that draws more than a dozen Winston Cup regulars. Skinner was so unprepared for what transpired that he literally had to cut out a copy of his sponsor's logo and hold it across the chest of his plain driver's uniform for the post-qualifying press conference.

That's when Childress called about the truck series opportunity, something Skinner turned down before calling Childress back and accepting the offer.

"It was too good an opportunity to let go by," Skinner said.

Being harnessed by such tight financial constraints forced

Skinner to make a deal with himself in regard to his future in NASCAR.

"I would have liked to have gotten started a little earlier," Skinner said. "I made myself a promise that I wouldn't go Winston Cup racing ever again if I couldn't go with a Richard Childress or a Rick Hendrick or a Richard Petty or a Jack Roush or somebody. I wanted to drive for one of the major forces in racing, and if I couldn't, I wasn't going to go."

He did take the offer, and he hasn't looked back, although he and Earnhardt suffered more than their share of injuries during the 1998 season.

Skinner crashed hard on April 5, 1998, at the Texas 500. But he returned a month and 10 days later to race at the Winston Open despite pain in his neck and shoulder. He also hurt his wrist and knee in the crash.

"That's the biggest problem we've faced this year," Childress said. "Mike Skinner took two of the most violent blows I've ever seen a driver take and still be walking. He's got to have operations this winter to get back in shape."

Skinner came back with a fourth-place finish at Indy in the Brickyard 400 Aug. 1, 1998, to silence his critics, many of whom wondered if he was the same driver since the crash.

"Maybe I can keep my job now. That would be cool," Skinner said at the time. "I'm trying to get back to health, trying to keep my job from being on the line, and days like today, with this whole team effort, make things much better and all worthwhile."

That knowledge of the "whole process" that Skinner brings will always be a big asset.

"There are times when Mike will come and spend a half day or three-quarters of the day here at the shop with the team, and that's very important," McReynolds said. "Mark Martin spends a lot of time with his team, and his performances on the racetrack are the result of that. A driver has to be an integral part of a team, and Mike is very much that with his team."

CHAPTER 23

TONY STEWART

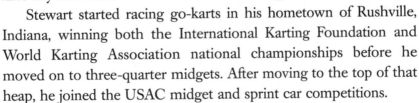

Stewart signs: Currently holds the fast lap record at the Indianapolis Motor Speedway for the new Indy Racing League cars; started on the pole for the 1996 Indianapolis 500; won the 1997 Indy Racing League Championship.

Tony Stewart is on the fast track, and with a move up to Joe Gibbs' Winston Cup team, don't look for Stewart to meander in the slow lane any time soon.

Stewart started racing go-karts in his hometown of Rushville, Indiana, winning both the International Karting Foundation and World Karting Association national championships before he moved on to three-quarter midgets. After moving to the top of that heap, he joined the USAC midget and sprint car competitions.

"I miss being on the dirt with the sprint cars. . . I don't get to run as many dirt events as I used to," Stewart said. "All the places we ran—Eldora and Terre Haute—we had a great time running there. So that's probably what I miss the most."

He won his first USAC National Midget Championship in 1994, and in 1995 became USAC's first driver to win the series' top three divisions—midget, sprint car and Silver Crown—in the same season.

From there, he took a part-time ride in the Busch Grand National series. When financing didn't work out there, he headed for the then-newly formed Indy Racing League, signing with Team Menard to compete in 1996.

In 1997, he kept up his IRL driving while joining Joe Gibbs' Shell Pontiac team on the Busch Grand National series. Some wondered whether he could do both rides, a thought Stewart quickly put to rest with his driving skills.

"I'm one of those guys that doesn't like it when somebody tells me I can't do something," said Stewart, who was born May 20, 1971. "This (BGN) series is so tough. When you go to a racetrack and have 45 cars qualify within three-tenths of a second, it is something no average Joe off the street can do. The cars are so even, and it puts so much pressure on the drivers. You've really got to be on your game."

What impressed Gibbs is that Stewart wanted to do things the right way from the very start, learning from Gibbs' top-driving Winston Cup and Busch Grand National veteran, Bobby Labonte.

"Here's what Tony said," Gibbs recalled. "He said, 'I don't think I'm ready to jump in a Winston Cup car. That's the big leagues over there. Yes, I've driven a lot of different types of cars, but I think I need time to work with a Busch car.' He got extremely excited about the opportunity to work with Bobby and having the chance to race in Busch."

Stewart said starting in Busch Grand National series made perfect sense.

"To come from the type of cars I come from that are half the weight, that's too much of a jump to assume you can just do that," Stewart said.

Coming back to NASCAR after a one-year break was not a tough decision.

"I think the challenge more than anything is why I wanted to come back," Stewart said. "I've driven a lot of different types of cars, and in most of them I've had a certain amount of success. I've struggled over here, and that really created a lot of drive in myself to challenge myself and see what I was lacking. That really pushes me to learn, and that takes a lot of the question marks out of my mind. It will help accelerate that learning curve. I thought it was a great opportunity to get with a quality team. This is a team that can push me forward and get me to learn what I need to get through the learning curve and come out a winner."

Labonte welcomed Stewart on board.

"I've seen a lot of talent throughout his career to know he's got a lot to bring to the table," Labonte said. "He might be past the 18 car. The 18 car might have to catch up to him eventually. We want that kind of challenge. Not a rivalry, but you want someone to help you push a little bit, and when he brings something to the table that's better than I can do, then I want to make it better. We want two potentially great race teams, not just one helping the other one."

Pontiac Motorsports manager Gary Claudio also saw Stewart's potential when he was signed for the 1997 BGN series.

"I first met this young man about a year and a half ago—I was extremely impressed with him," Claudio said at the time. "To have him in a Pontiac for a short time, then lose him, and now have him back again is just marvelous. I think the future is his to be had. Working with tutors like Jimmy Makar and Bobby Labonte and Coach Gibbs is just marvelous. When Joe first told me he was working on Tony Stewart, I couldn't get the smile off my face. To get this young man in with the team he has already in place is really an accomplishment. It's just great for Pontiac. I'm in a great position to accept this team into Pontiac.

"Bobby and Tony are the future of Winston Cup. They are it, believe me. These gentlemen will be heard from. I think when you have an opportunity to get a team like this, and get a type of driver like Tony, then you have to go for it. I went to my people and said, 'Look, this opportunity may come to fruition, and if it does, we're going to have to be prepared to step up.' We're committed to the 18 car, and they've shown in a very short time what they can do in a Pontiac. I'm looking forward to even better things with this new organization that Tony's joining. Whatever monetary amount is involved is really going to pay dividends down the road."

Stewart credits Gibbs with making the transition easy in a lot of ways.

"There is no real easy way to describe Joe other than he is an absolute joy to work with," Stewart said. "His leadership qualities are what keep everyone going. He knows his role as a car owner, he knows his people, how to keep everything flowing. Even when we have a bad day, Joe has a magical way of getting us pumped up and making us feel like we can do anything. He's a great leader. There have been days when we've had a rough day in qualifying and the race team wasn't feeling real good. We're sitting in the trailer thinking, 'Well, we can at least try to stay on the lead lap.' Then Joe will give his morning speech before the race, and you feel like you're going to lap the field a few times. He is probably the easiest guy I've ever worked with as a car owner. He's very easy to get along with. He doesn't ask a lot. He just asks you to go out and do your job and represent the company well."

The Busch Series was a big adjustment at first. "This has been by far the hardest division to make the transition into," Stewart said. "These cars are twice as heavy as anything I've ever driven. They have harder tires than anything I've ever driven. It's been a big challenge running on the radial (tires) and learning all the racetracks. The Busch Series and Cup Series—there's nothing easy about either one of them. You've got 50 guys here that are all capable of getting in the show. They all fall so close that when you get here, you'd better be prepared. Competing in the Busch Series challenges your versatility as a driver. You have to be able to quickly make track adjustments to get the car up to speed in order to qualify. With the level of competition in the Busch Series at an all-time high, it's critical for us to get a good starting spot."

He also is grateful to Labonte.

"Bobby has done so much getting me re-acclimated to running a stock car," Stewart said. "No matter how busy he is on the weekend, he always takes the time to come over to our garage and find out how everything is going, to ask us if there is anything that he can help with. He's been a tremendous asset, very generous, and on top of that he's become a very good friend. He's a motivator."

The ones who helped get Stewart into racing are outside of NASCAR, but very much into racing.

"I would say my father and an ex-teammate of mine, Mark Dismore in the IRL Series, helped encourage my racing career the most. Between my father and Mark, they are the two guys who have taught me just about everything I know. My father and I went to a go-kart race in Westport, Indiana, in 1979. About a month later we had our own racing kart, and we started running on the little dirt tracks in Indiana with a go-kart. My father was involved in racing, and as far back as I can remember, that's all I was interested in," Stewart said. "My father took me to a lot of races, and I think from the first time I was at a race and actually knew what I was watching, I knew that was what I wanted to do for the rest of my life."

Making the change to stock cars required a lot of track time.

"The biggest difference is with the Indy car, they are half the weight of a stock car, with all the advantages of front and rear wings and aerodynamics that plant the car on the track," Stewart said. "When you go to a stock car, it is twice as heavy, wider tires, much less down force. You have to be much more patient with a stock car, and not overdrive the car. The first time you drive them it takes some time to learn how it reacts. But it's kind of like a bicycle, once you've been on one, you don't really forget how it works. Once you get back in it, you get re-acclimated. It just takes a couple of laps."

Running the IRL (Indy Racing League) and BGN (Busch Grand National) series in 1997 gave Stewart little free time. Moving up to the Winston Cup Series full time in 1999 will mean even more commitments both on and off the track.

"The changes have been mainly in the schedule; with all the traveling we do, I don't have the personal time at home with my friends. When I do come home, my friends and I go out to dinner. We have a lot of fun when people come up and ask for autographs. That's something different; we didn't used to have a lot of that. Normally, I have four-wheelers I ride with my friends. Just spending time with my family and friends at home, trying to catch up is the most important thing I do with my free time."

The hard work needed to succeed in NASCAR means constantly attaining goals, and setting even higher goals.

"We never want to stop setting goals, and we never want to set a limit. We want to get in every race we can; we want to win every race we can, and we want to be champions in every series we run. Of course, the Daytona 500 and the Indianapolis 500 are two main goals, but we always want more; we won't stop there," he said.

Stewart tells his young fans to set high goals but keep a perspective.

"Don't give up, first of all. Be realistic with your goals," Stewart said. "Not everyone will be the next Jeff Gordon or Dale Earnhardt or Rick Mears or A.J. Foyt. Work your way up the ladder, through each rank, and be patient. A lot of times when people try and make a move that they are not ready for, that's what stops their careers. So take your time, be patient and work very hard."

Being from Indiana, Stewart likes his home state's premier track.

"I think the Indianapolis Motor Speedway is the most unique track I've ever been on," Stewart said. "But my favorites are probably Phoenix International Raceway, Indianapolis Raceway Park, Eldora Speedway in Ohio, and probably the Chili Bowl in Tulsa, Oklahoma."

All drivers have their own particular likes and dislikes in terms of car setup.

"Normally, if anything we try to keep the car a little bit tight. I find it keeps me out of a little bit of trouble during the race. If the car is tight, you can drive it more with the throttle, and if it is loose, you have to do a little more backsteering than throttle. So if we have a choice, we like to keep it a little more on the tight side."

NASCAR's continuing surge in popularity is amazing, even to Stewart.

"Really, I don't have an answer for that," Stewart said. "To a certain degree it's that you have so many American-based cars and drivers on the series. You don't see foreign drivers, and you have an everyday battle with Ford and Chevrolet and Pontiac. To be able to see 42 guys battle it out, duel it out each weekend is exciting. And it's more fun, from my perspective anyway, than watching a baseball game or some guy chase a golf ball around. More people are finding out about the sport, and it's a great sport, and that's what makes it grow."

Stewart now has his sights set on the Winston Cup.

"Hopefully, if my career can grow in five years as much as Joe Gibbs' career has grown in five years in NASCAR, then we can have a Winston Cup championship," Stewart said. "But for now we are just going to concentrate on growing as a team, placing well in races and being consistent, moving up in the points standings and putting ourselves in a position to win races. We would like to win championships like everyone else, but we have to be realistic at the same time."

Some fans might think drivers who come to the NASCAR scene from the open-wheel leagues get a cool reception. Stewart claims the NASCAR drivers have been great to him.

"It seems like we got a pretty fair reception," Stewart said. "I don't have too many of the guys that I don't get along with. I pretty much get along with everybody right now."

He also knows that qualifying will be very important—you can't win if you don't make the field.

"Everybody is so competitive that you can't afford to be a tenth or two-tenths off in qualifying," Stewart said. "You've really got to be on top of the game and know every inch of the racetrack. The biggest step is just to try to make each race—try to make sure we're not going home on Saturday night instead of Sunday night. And once we've made the race, then we just need to finish every lap we can finish. We just need experience the first year—for every lap that we get in the race, there's no way you can possibly get that kind of experience in testing, and there's no dollar amount that can replace that. Right now the biggest thing is we just want to make the races and finish as many races as we can. Realistically, we just want to make the shows. The Winston Cup series is the toughest series in America right now, if not in the world. So to come into the series and expect to go out and win races the first year, I think that's being pretty crazy right now."

Gibbs knows the Winston Cup success won't come overnight, even for a driver as talented as Stewart.

"I went back and looked at everybody from Jeff Gordon to Dale Earnhardt in their first years," Gibbs said. "It's a tough, long, hard fight. We know that's what we're in for. There's going to be some hard lumps and bruises in there when you step up to Winston Cup. We know that. We're ready for it. So we're geared for the long haul. We know it's not going to be an easy journey."

The season in the Busch series should help Stewart in the Winston Cup competitions.

"To be able to go to those tracks and run up front is something that definitely builds some confidence," Stewart said. "But we know it's going to be much more difficult when we make the move up. That's why we're thankful to get this track time now in the Busch cars."

And with Home Depot sponsoring his Winston Cup ride, Stewart joked that at least he has the building materials to put things back together should the need arise.

"I'm looking forward to it," Stewart said. "It's hard to get into Winston Cup racing, and there's dues to be paid. I'm sure I'm going to bend a lot of sheet metal. But at least with Home Depot, we've got two-by-fours and nails we can use to put it back together."

CHAPTER 24

DARRELL WALTRIP

On Waltrip's wall: Three-time NASCAR Winston Cup champion while driving for Junior Johnson; winner of inaugural running of the Winston in 1985 at Charlotte Motor Speedway; became team owner as well as driver in 1991, two years after winning 1989 Daytona 500 in his 17th try; has 84 career victories.

Don't ever say "never" when it comes to Darrell Waltrip.

Waltrip was struggling when 1998 began, but in 1999 he was signed to drive the K-Mart Ford Taurus and team with Cup stand-out Jimmy Spencer.

Waltrip won the Winston Cup Series points title in 1981, 1982 and 1985. His first NASCAR Winston Cup Series start was in 1972 at the Winston 500—but he would not get his first win until three years later in his 50th start. In 1981, Waltrip won eight races from the pole, including four straight. After he won the 1989 Daytona 500, he celebrated with a shuffling two-step dance that is part of NASCAR folklore.

The 1996 season was a near disaster. In 1997 Waltrip was struggling as an owner and driver and was only 26th in the point standings. There was a lot of uncertainty surrounding Waltrip in 1998. But when rookie Steve Park was injured, the owner of Park's car, the No. 1 Pennzoil, called—it was Dale Earnhardt, asking Waltrip if he'd like to sub.

"This is a perfect example of why you should never say never," Waltrip said. "The last person in the world I ever thought I would be driving for was Dale Earnhardt. But this is a win-win situation for everyone involved. It gives Dale Earnhardt Inc. and Pennzoil some stability; now that all the headaches of being a team owner are behind me, I'm ready to climb into the Pennzoil Monte Carlo and prove to everyone that Darrell Waltrip can still get the job done as a race car driver."

"I think everybody wins with this deal," Earnhardt said. "I'm excited about having Darrell in there to help my team grow. We're brand new, and we got all frazzled when Steve got hurt. This gives us some confidence."

Waltrip was 15th at Talladega in April, and then really heated up when he took fifth place in the California 500 presented by NAPA the first week in May.

"You cannot imagine all that I have been through this year, and then for this to happen today is hard for even someone like me to put into words," Waltrip said after the California race. "I knew this team could win, and you saw today just how close we are. There's still some fire in the old belly, and I'm with a crowd that wants to win. They believe in me, and I believe in them. Perseverance and hard work, that will always pay off, and that's the secret to everything. Dale Earnhardt gave me a lot of confidence. He called me and said, 'I want you to drive this car because I know you can win in this car.' That meant a lot to me. It doesn't get better than this. I have never been in a situation like this in my life, not since the Junior Johnson days."

Waltrip put together four straight top-20 finishes in the No. 2 Pennzoil Monte Carlo. How could he top that? Easy. Waltrip went to Michigan in June and took 12th at the Miller Lite 400 at Michigan Speedway. He was so intent on making the top 10 that initially, he couldn't acknowledge the accomplishment.

"That wasn't great, but it was pretty good," Waltrip said as he climbed from the Pennzoil Monte Carlo. Then seconds later he smiled and added, "You know, that was actually really good."

Had enough? Waltrip hadn't. He went to Long Pond, Pennsylvania, in the third week of June and pulled off a sixth-place finish at Pocono in the Pocono 500.

"You know, a whole lot of people buried ol' D.W., but I guess they just didn't put enough dirt on me because I'm still alive, and I'm crawling out of a hole," Waltrip said. "I've been in some holes in my life, but today I'm feeling about as happy as I have in a long time. This means so much that it is hard to put into words. This has given me new life."

Waltrip posted a 13th-place finish the following week at Sears Point in the Save Mart/Kragen 350. While Park came back soon after and resumed his spot in the No. 1 Pennzoil, Waltrip still drove respectably in the No. 35 Tabasco for the rest of the 1998 season.

"I'd say the biggest thing Darrell helped us out on was realizing our potential," said No. 1 Pennzoil crew chief Philippe Lopez. "We struggled a bit at the beginning, but when he came in, he was able to bring our cars home, and we could work on the race cars. Then our finishes got better and better. It's really important to have someone who can take care of equipment like that."

More memories for Waltrip, a driver who already has a truck full of racing memories:

"One of the fondest races I can remember was in '79 when I beat Richard (Petty) in Darlington; we swapped the lead a couple times, and I beat him back to the line," Waltrip said. "I won the Winston and chased Harry down and caught him on the last lap and won the first Winston. I made up four laps at Richmond and beat Lenny Pond, did the same thing at Martinsville and won. These were all in the late '70s. All the wins with Junior were incredible, to come back from adversity to win. In '89, winning the Daytona 500, that was a big thrill, but it just worked out. A couple weeks later in Atlanta I had to hold off a couple guys to win, and the World 600 that year was a tough one that I won."

Waltrip was only 30 years old when he beat the likes of Richard Petty, Bobby Allison and David Pearson in 1977 for his first NASCAR Winston Cup superspeedway win, capitalizing on a wreck up front and gunning the throttle to make it to the caution first—which was crucial, since the green flag never came back out.

"It was my first chance to say, 'Hey boys, I'm here and you're going to have to deal with me,'" says Waltrip, who first challenged Darlington in 1973. "With the toughness of Darlington, winning it showed I had arrived as a driver. It proved my previous wins on short tracks were no flukes.

"I knew that if you were ever going to prove yourself in this business, you had to win Darlington. Winning Darlington makes people take you seriously. There was a perception that nobody could beat those guys. They were the sport, and no one else mattered. It made it fun beating them. I probably would not have won if not for the wreck, but I did. Nothing can change that. I think it helped put the name of Darrell Waltrip in another category. There was a field of drivers who had pretty much been around the sport since its inception. It was kind of exciting when a new guy would show up with a car nobody had ever seen before with a sponsor nobody had ever heard of before and get out there and actually be competitive and make the field—that was big."

In 1979, Waltrip beat Richard Petty. The two battled, each taking the lead four times in the final lap before Waltrip nudged out the King for the checkered flag at Darlington.

"You can never get too comfortable at Darlington," Waltrip said. "I proved that. At that point in the race, I thought I was in a nice, cozy recliner, but in actuality, I was in an office chair with wild wheels. Do I respect the place? You better believe it. And for anyone else who wants to win at that tough ol' track, they better, too. Tell them to ask ol' D.W. about it."

"The one that got away" from Waltrip was the 1979 points title.

"I could kick my rear a thousand times for not winning the 1979 Winston Cup championship. I gave it away. I just blew it. I wasn't in it by myself, but still, I was the quarterback and the captain of the ship and let that one slip through the cracks. But nevertheless, I learned a lot from it.

"I've anguished over that through all the years. I still anguish over that. I was so determined to beat Richard Petty. It was my chance to dethrone the King. I was being compared to Richard, compared to David (Pearson), better than Richard, better than David. I had this chance to take advantage of that and prove everybody was right. Then I blew it. That was really, really hard on me at that point in time."

Others have volunteered to "kick" Waltrip's rear on occasion—although just in jest, because Waltrip truly is a living legend.

"Well, certainly Richard in the late 1970s and David (Pearson) and Bobby Allison in the 1980s; Earnhardt, (Bill) Elliott and Rusty (Wallace) in the middle or latter part of the '80s—up until Gordon came along—those were my rivals," Waltrip said. "Bobby and I ended up in some pretty heated battles in '81, '82 and '83. That obviously left a tremendous impression on him. I never knew he disliked me so much. I always thought he was kidding, but apparently he wasn't. He doesn't like me, but I love him. I have no ill feelings toward him at all. I have nothing but compassion for Bobby. We had run-ins on the racetrack but that was then and this is now. We were racing and you can't hold a grudge all your life for something that happened on a racetrack."

Waltrip asked his family about racing when he was younger.

"Believe it or not, my grandmother and grandfather exposed me to the sport," Waltrip said. "And G.C. Spencer, a driver in the late '60s and '70s from Owensboro. G.C. was a really great driver. But my grandparents would take me to the races on Sunday, sitting up there watching those cars going around. I can remember being 6 years old and telling my grandmother that's what I wanted to do. I never lost that dream; I kept pursuing it. Through go-karts, hobby cars, Modified, NASCAR Sportsman cars, then Busch Grand National and into the Winston Cup. It's a long and winding road, and you can get there if you don't give up.

"There was absolutely no reason, no background in my family, to have the success I've had. I just wanted it," Waltrip said.

"One of my proudest accomplishments or involvements is Motor Racing Outreach, MRO," Waltrip said. "Lake Speed, Bobby Hillin, our wives and I started it with Max Helton. It has been the glue to our racing family. We've had some tough times with friends passing. To have everyone help, to have NASCAR endorse and give us time and space to hold Sunday services is one of my proudest moments."

Forays into broadcasting have been fun for Waltrip—and for the fans, who tell him wherever he goes how much they enjoy his television commentary.

"I personally think I was made for television," Waltrip said. "With my personality and the way I like to express things, television is a good avenue for fans to see who I really am. It's a good opportunity for fans to see more than just the guy who drives. They get to see more than just the guy who's banging out there, who has a great wife and two great kids.

"I love TV. I love the fans. I think I have the insight to help people understand. It's kind of interesting at 50 years old to be talking about where my future lies. I'm going to give my race team everything I've got for the next year or so. I've got my eyes wide open for a guy who I can take under my wings and build for the future, but right now, that guy just doesn't seem available. Hopefully, I've also been able to help some people and inspire some people. But at 50, I sometimes don't feel too good, but I also think that there are still some wins out there for me."

Although he only became a TV commentator in recent years, Waltrip has always been well aware of the potential of the electronic media.

"I've always been a fan of TV, even before I was standing in front of the camera," Waltrip said. "I always liked talking to the media; I thought it was cool to go home and see yourself on the TV. I never thought that would happen. I love doing the television commentary. I feel very comfortable doing it. I don't want to totally give up driving because it gives me so much insight. When I can go on the track, then take that experience in the booth, I can really share a lot with the fans that the other guys can't. Plus, I really like to make a fool of myself, and if I'm going to do that, I like a big audience."

The goal for Waltrip is simple: Running the races is no longer enough, he must return to the high level he drove for so long.

"I know in my heart and my mind that I can still win a race," Waltrip said. "We just need to get the car like I need it and the team like I need it. The one thing that I've been disappointed with is that I haven't been a factor for the Winston Cup."

His time as an owner is something that Waltrip doesn't remember all too fondly.

"Being the owner and the driver, yeah, that's a distraction," Waltrip said. "That's a very tough road to hoe, so to speak. Where the difficulty comes is dealing with people, separating the roles. The driver role has to have the crew be his buddies and eat with them and things. But when the driver has to come out of the role and become their boss—that's where there are problems. Because of that you can make some bad business decisions. You hire people because you like them; you won't fire someone because they'll have a tough time without the job. That's the part I've struggled with. It's hard for a driver to look at profits and losses. I've been told, and I know it's true, that I have a driver's mentality, which isn't a negative. That means I think like a driver, not an owner. It's difficult for me to accept as the team owner, I've got no problems driving, but I do have problems being the team owner."

Part of the problem nowadays is that with the competitive level being so high, sponsors and drivers are looking for success sooner rather than later.

"In all honesty, one of the problems we have in this sport is that it's very difficult to find the people or the sponsors who'll give you the time to develop something," Waltrip said. "They want results, now. That's why I've had some problems the last few years. As I say that, I look at my truck team who had a great year in 1997. The season was hardly over when my driver told me he was leaving to find a full-time Winston Cup ride. He deserved it, and I wish I would have been able to provide him one. Almost at the same time, my sponsor, DieHard, told me they had invested as much time into a team as they wanted. So, I thought up to that point that performance was the issue, but now it doesn't seem that way. There aren't a lot of sponsors out there who are willing to wait. That's why it's hard to go out there and find the new young superstar, the next Jeff Gordon, because sponsors don't have the patience to understand that it could take a couple of years. So that may have an impact on whether I stay on the owner side of things after I'm done driving."

Waltrip became a complete person when he found the Lord.

"My faith is where I get my strength these days," Waltrip said. "I drove for so many years pleasing myself, pleasing my peers. I drove very selfishly. In 1983 or so, when I gave my life to the Lord, there started to be changes in my life. And now it's a very important part of my life. It affects decisions I make; it affects the way I feel, the way I act. I've been pleased that I've been able to change my way of life and have the fans respect it. That's not why I did it, but it's nice. My involvement with Motor Racing Outreach is an important part of my life right now, as well as my involvement with my children and my family. I don't drive my car to please myself anymore. I don't drive to please fans or sponsors, or whatever. I drive as hard as I can to please the Lord. I want my children to see me win races, like I did 15 years ago. I want them to be proud of their dad and what he does for a living. But one valuable lesson I learned is that if you're going to live and die by winning and losing, then you're going to die a lot. I just feel like my role has changed, just like the sponsors we're looking at. They're not the ones I would have chosen, but they're ones that have come to me."

That faith has Waltrip certain about what he should be thankful for: his wife, Stevie, and their children.

"Being in the room when Jessica was born and cutting the cord and that whole thing, I mean, that was such a bonding moment for Stevie and me," Waltrip said. "I mean, we loved each other, and we always have. We've been close, but when I was in there with her and she was having that baby . . . the whole thing, it was so emotional. I had a lot of respect for her before then, but I had a totally new respect for her after that."

Five years after doctors said she'd never have another child, 42-year-old Stevie had Sarah Kaitlyn.

"We have to give God every bit of the credit for having Jessica and Sarah Kaitlyn," Stevie said. "Darrell and I both had problems (having kids). And then our age was against us, too, because I was 37 when I had Jessica. So we had nothing in our favor. All we had was God. And He did it. It's just a neat story."

Waltrip hopes other folks see the deep relationship many Winston Cup drivers have with the Lord and take part of that into their own hearts.

"I would like to say that I've seen Jeff Gordon and others give the Lord praise for their victories," Waltrip said. "And I've heard people wonder if they thought they were chosen or something. That's not why we do it. It's just to bring praise to his name. None of us Christians believe we're any better than others, we just need to praise him. Unless you have Jesus in your heart, and you understand that relationship, you wouldn't understand why someone praises Jesus for the win or for their safety."

Also, in regard to Gordon, Waltrip claims the driver of the No. 24 car has been dominating in a time when the sport is hard to dominate.

"I think the biggest thing today is the way the sport is officiated," Waltrip said. "It makes it very difficult for anyone to get an advantage. I know people are going to say, 'What about Jeff Gordon?' I think that team represents what can happen when you've got a great crew chief, unlimited funds and a very talented driver. It's like I was long ago, I was the best driver with the best owner and the best team. We had Junior Johnson, the most money and the best team. We parlayed that into win after win after win and into championships. His timing is perfect, just like mine was."

The racing game has become more mechanical as technology has evolved.

"But when you monitor everything as closely as NASCAR does today, and parity being the operative word week in and week out—parity is what has made our sport different than when I was dominating," Waltrip said. "Then, you could carry your team. Today, it's more in-depth, the guy who can fine-tune his car. It's the guy who can get another tenth out of his car. You do that with technology. When I was winning it was more up to the driver. Now its more up to the car and the race itself. Obviously, keeping the cars balanced is key in NASCAR's eyes, but it makes it difficult to dominate—unless you have a driver like Jeff Gordon."

Although Gordon seems to be the brunt of some negative behavior from fans, Waltrip respects the young champion.

"If Jeff Gordon was as outspoken as I was, he would basically be following in my footsteps," Waltrip said. "He's just come into the sport and is beating the heroes who have established themselves in this sport over the past 10 years or so. I sympathize with him to some degree. Fortunately for him, he's usually not one to say the wrong thing. He usually says the politically correct thing, which I think just comes from watching people like me make big fools out of themselves. He's learning not to do that. But nevertheless, part of my outspokenness was intentional, part of it was unintentional. Part of that was promoted by those around me who knew that I loved to run my mouth and was pretty clever, had a great sense of humor and could have a lot of fun. Even if I wasn't entertaining anyone but myself, I was having fun doing it. Part of that was by design, but a lot of it got blown out of proportion because I allowed it to, rather than stepping back and saying, 'Whoa! Time out! This is not going like I wanted it to.'

"The difference between then and now is that the cars are so much better now," Waltrip said. "Power steering, bias tires, wind-tunnel testing on the cars are much different from 10-20 years ago when I was dominating the sport. Today's racing has totally different concepts, totally different approaches. Easier? Yeah, I think it's easier—if you get a car that's right. The drivers have it a little easier now.